B291
Financial accounting

The Open University

Business School

Unit 6

Accountants, auditing, ethics and governance

Written by Devendra Kodwani

Module Team

Dr Devendra Kodwani, *B291 Chair & Author*

Dr Carien van Mourik, *Author*

Professor Jane Frecknall-Hughes, *Professional Certificate in Accounting Chair & Author*

Catherine Gowthorpe, *Author*

Kelly Dobbs, *Curriculum Assistant*

Elizabeth R Porter, *Regional Manager*

Sam Cooper, *Programme Coordinator*

Emir Forken, *Qualifications Manager*

Dr Lesley Messer, *Programme Manager*

Funmi Mapelujo, *Curriculum Manager*

External Assessor

Professor Stuart Turley, Manchester Business School

Critical Readers

Professor Judy Day, Manchester Business School

Elizabeth R Porter

Professor Peter Walton

Developmental Testers

Dr Teodora Burnand

Sam Cooper

Vimal Goricha

Vani Shri Goswami

Dudley Hughes

Production Team

Martin Brazier, *Graphic Designer*

Anne Brown, *Media Assistant*

Sarah Cross, *Print Buyer*

Beccy Dresden, *Media Project Manager*

Vicky Eves, *Graphic Artist*

Paul Hoffman, *Editor*

Diane Hopwood, *Rights Assistant*

Lucinda Simpson, *Editor*

Kelvin Street, *Library*

Software

Accounting package software was designed by and remains the property of Sage plc.

Other Material

The Module Team wishes to acknowledge use of some material from B680 *The Certificate in Accounting*.

This publication forms part of the Open University module B291 *Financial accounting*. Details of this and other Open University modules can be obtained from the Student Registration and Enquiry Service, The Open University, PO Box 197, Milton Keynes MK7 6BJ, United Kingdom (tel. +44 (0)845 300 60 90; email general-enquiries@open.ac.uk).

Alternatively, you may visit the Open University website at www.open.ac.uk where you can learn more about the wide range of modules and packs offered at all levels by The Open University.

To purchase a selection of Open University materials visit www.ouw.co.uk, or contact Open University Worldwide, Walton Hall, Milton Keynes MK7 6AA, United Kingdom for a brochure (tel. +44 (0)1908 858793; fax +44 (0)1908 858787; email ouw-customer-services@open.ac.uk).

The Open University

Walton Hall

Milton Keynes

MK7 6AA

First published 2010. Second edition 2012.

Edited and designed by The Open University.

Typeset in India by OKS Prepress Services, Chennai.

Printed in the United Kingdom by Henry Ling Limited, at the Dorset Press, Dorchester, DT1 1HD.

ISBN 978 1 7800 7378 1

2.1

Contents

Introduction

In the previous five units you learned why and how financial statements are produced. In this unit we want you to stand back from the 'how' part of accounting and re-engage with the 'why' part, so we will be discussing a set of wider issues and the context of accounting to which Unit 1 briefly referred.

In Unit 1 you learned that financial reports are used by a diverse set of users, internal and external to business enterprise. These stakeholders rely on information contained in financial statements to help them make many important decisions. For example, current and prospective investors use information provided in an income statement and balance sheet to decide whether they should invest or not in an enterprise. Similarly, suppliers, tax authorities, bankers, customers and government, environmental groups and many other interested individuals and institutions rely on financial statements to form their judgements about many aspects of a business entity. This unit addresses issues related to business ethics, corporate governance, corporate social responsibility and audit. The main objective is to make you aware of how these wider issues underpin the practice of accounting and the role that accountants are expected to play.

As was explained in Unit 1, professionally qualified accountants and auditors function in a regulatory and legal environment. The legal environment comprises tax law, company law and many other regulations that require accounting practitioners to follow certain rules and regulations. The professional environment also comprises professional codes of conduct and governance codes that require accountants to perform their functions with integrity and competence. An important job that qualified auditors (who are themselves usually qualified accountants) perform is auditing the books prepared by other accountants. The purpose of auditing is to provide an opinion on the financial statements, stating whether they show a true and fair view of the financial position of the company. These accounting and auditing responsibilities require not only understanding of the legal context but also of the wider issues of ethics and corporate social responsibility. These issues are addressed in greater detail in this unit.

In Units 2 and 3 you learned about the process of recording transactions and other events. Although, as you learned in these units, the process of recording information in books of accounts is guided by the principles and conventions of accounting, there are many areas where accountants have to make choices in that process. For example, you learned in Unit 3 that long-term assets (non-current assets), such as machinery, are depreciated over the useful economic life of the asset so that depreciation expense is matched to revenues earned in a particular accounting period. However, there is some degree of subjectivity and judgement involved in determining the amount of depreciation. Estimates have to be made about the length of useful economic life, the appropriate depreciation method and the residual value of the asset at the end of its useful economic life. This means, depending on different estimates, a different depreciation expense could be charged in an accounting period for assets of the same type. Also, these estimates and depreciation expenses will not necessarily be the same for different companies. This in turn has an effect on the profit or loss reported for the period. Thus it is seen that accounting does involve making choices and is not a purely mechanical process. In this unit you will learn about the implications of such accounting-related choices from the perspectives of ethics and governance.

Unit 6 consists of the following five inter-related sessions.

Session 1 introduces you to the ethical issues that arise in the context of business and accounting and to a conceptual framework to deal with ethical dilemmas.

Session 2 explores corporate governance as a development meant to ensure that the management of public limited companies operates in the interests of key stakeholders, such as providers of capital.

Session 3 discusses various aspects of corporate governance, ethics and corporate social responsibility, along with legal issues.

Session 4 provides an understanding of the purpose and scope of internal and external auditing.

Session 5 discusses the issues of fraud and fraud detection and the auditor's responsibility with respect to the prevention of fraud.

Learning aims and outcomes of Unit 6

Upon completion of Unit 6 you are expected to be able to:
1   understand and discuss ethics and professional values in the context of accounting
2   explain the need to comply with ethical, professional and regulatory frameworks
3   discuss the need for and the scope of corporate governance
4   explain the relationship between ethics, governance, the law and social responsibility
5   explain the role and functions of internal and external auditing
6   explain the need for and process of preventing accounting-related frauds.

SESSION **1 Ethics in business and accounting**

Introduction

Upon completion of Session 1 you should be able to:

* understand the meaning of ethics in general and business contexts
* explain different approaches to accounting ethics
* understand professional codes of ethics
* understand and use a conceptual framework to deal with ethical dilemmas.

In Session 1 you will learn about the meaning of business ethics and why ethics are important in business and to the accounting profession. The session will introduce different approaches to accounting ethics and describe the codes of ethics that professional accounting bodies expect professionally qualified accountants to follow. The session then describes a conceptual framework to deal with ethical dilemmas.

1.1 The meaning of ethics

Consider a hypothetical business situation given below in Activity 1.1 and then respond to the question.

Activity 1.1

A leading footwear company gets its branded shoes made in an economically developing country and sells those shoes in economically more developed countries. It has emerged that the suppliers of shoes from the developing country use the services of children as young as 12 years old and pay them minimum wages, as per the law of that country. It is also known that income earned by the majority of such children supports their families, who would otherwise have problems in obtaining adequate income. There is no law in the developing country that prohibits the employment of children.

Would you consider it ethical behaviour to buy the shoes that have been sourced from suppliers in the developing country? Provide reasons to support your answer. (Spend no more than ten minutes on this activity.)

Feedback

You may argue that buying the shoes from the company in question is an unethical decision simply because young children should not be put to work and deprived of their childhood, even though it seems that it is not illegal in the given situation. This argument takes an absolutist ethical viewpoint that child labour should not be employed in any circumstances.

Alternatively, you may argue that children's employment in the above situation protects the dependent families against possible malnutrition and starvation, hence employing children is ethically right in such a situation. This argument takes a relativist view, considering the consequences of the action and weighing the costs and benefits.

There could be another view that child labour is perhaps acceptable in the short term until the developing country achieves higher income levels. All these arguments are underpinned by some ethical standpoint that a respondent has taken. Perhaps your answer was supported by different arguments. This shows that ethical dilemmas may produce different responses from different individuals and clear guidelines or rules to deal with ethical dilemmas may not be possible in practice.

Activity 1.1 illustrates that from an individual's perspective an ethical dilemma could be evaluated using different viewpoints. The situation described illustrates the difference between a legal position and an ethical position. While it may be legal to hire child labour in a particular country it may still be considered unethical, depending on what an individual thinks about the rights of children.

Now consider the issue from the perspective of a business enterprise. Business enterprises are different from individual consumers in the sense that business enterprises generally exist to make profits. Consider again the illustrative situation in Activity 1.1: should the footwear company source its supplies from a supplier who hires children in an economically developing country? Clearly a situation such as that described in Activity 1.1 forces us to consider issues that are beyond any legal position and pushes us into a philosophical domain, searching for the meaning of ethics.

1.1.1 Definition of ethics

The literal meaning of ethics originally implied common practices and customs. The Greek term *ethic* merely meant manners. According to philosopher Peter Singer (1985), ethics means 'the systematic study of what we ought to do'. Ethics deals with the question of what is morally good and bad, right and wrong. Peter Singer further explains that morality and ethics are closely related. However, making a fine distinction, he says that ethics is not morality itself but a field of study that has morality as its subject matter. Hence, according to Singer, 'ethics is equivalent to moral philosophy'. While we could go into much greater detail about the meaning of ethics and morality and the differences between them, we will restrict the discussion here. Those interested in pursuing this further could start with the excellent write up by Peter Singer (1985). Our purpose here is to highlight that ethics are being discussed as a backdrop to corporate governance, accounting and auditing. Hence, we do not intend to go into a philosophical debate on this topic. The words 'ethics' and 'morality' are used interchangeably in this module.

In the illustration provided in Activity 1.1, what would be the 'good' or 'right' decision? In the feedback one of the arguments put forward is that child labour is not acceptable, irrespective of legality. This absolute view implies a universal ethical statement, which needs no further justification other than the claim that children under a certain age should not be working because it is not a good practice in society. Contrast this with the view that children could be generating income that supports the family. This latter view, also called the consequentialist view, considers the consequences of an action when faced with ethical dilemma. If an individual considers that letting children work is a universally bad idea then that individual will find that child labour is an unacceptable idea. So what should guide our individual choices? Should these be our own views on the morality of an action (taking into account the consequences) or should we be guided by some universal ideals? If it is the latter, who should define the universal ideals for moral behaviour? It is not possible in this module and in this unit to answer these questions, but in personal and professional life situations we often have to deal with these questions. Here we will refer back to Singer's view, which suggests that ethical judgements are not to be viewed solely from personal viewpoints and considerations. Singer (1997) takes the view 'that [the] distinguishing feature of ethics is that ethical judgements are universalisable. Ethics requires us to go beyond our own personal point of view to a standpoint like that of the impartial spectator who takes a universal point of view.'

1.1.2 Business ethics

Considering the above brief explanation of ethics, what does business ethics mean? You may argue that a business enterprise, particularly a corporate entity, is a legal entity and as such does not have any values or morals of its own. This argument holds true only if you can establish that the ethics of those working in the corporation do not affect their decisions and behaviour in relation to their jobs. Such separation of individual or group ethics from business decisions seems an unrealistic assumption. Business entities are subject to relevant laws such as contract law, company law and many other relevant rules and regulations of the country in which they operate. In addition, companies incorporated under the companies legislation in the UK operate under the powers and responsibilities conferred by the Memorandum and Articles of Association. Business organisations also adopt voluntary codes of conduct and have to comply with many other corporate governance requirements. All these voluntary, legal and social constraints on business may require a business entity to abide by certain ethical codes. There is no universally accepted definition of business ethics, but here is one definition that may be useful:

> standards businesses should observe in their dealings over and above compliance with the letter of the law. This covers questions such as fair dealing with their labour force, customers, suppliers, and competitors, and the impact of their activities on the environment, public health, and animal welfare.
>
> (Black et al., 2009)

The above definition clearly points out that ethical standards go beyond the legal requirements of conducting business. An ethical business enterprise, therefore, is expected to be fair in its dealing with various stakeholders and so must go beyond compliance with legal requirements when taking decisions that affect various stakeholders as well as the environment. Applying this definition to the situation described in Activity 1.1, it could be argued that if the business enterprise operates in a society where businesses are expected to source their supplies from those suppliers who do not employ children, then the business firm will need to abide by such social norms. In general, business firms not only try to meet these expectations but also consciously pursue the business practices that are deemed ethically appropriate in a given society. For example, some supermarkets in the UK sell goods such as tea, coffee or fruits bearing the Fairtrade mark. This mark indicates that the suppliers of goods were paid fair prices for their produce. The Fairtrade Foundation is a not-for-profit voluntary organisation that describes its view of fair trade as follows:

> Fairtrade is about better prices, decent working conditions, local sustainability, and fair terms of trade for farmers and workers in the developing world. By requiring companies to pay sustainable prices (which must never fall lower than the market price), Fairtrade addresses the injustices of conventional trade, which traditionally discriminates against the poorest, weakest producers. It enables them to improve their position and have more control over their lives.
>
> (Fairtrade Foundation, 2010)

The above explanation of fair trade illustrates aspects of business that could be subject to ethical appreciation or criticism. The position taken by the Fairtrade Foundation that 'conventional trade' is not just and that conventional business enterprise 'discriminates against the poorest, weakest producers' is debatable. We could also argue about what is sustainable or about market price in this context. Mainstream economics suggest that in free markets the price coordinates production and consumption decisions. Any attempt to bring into consideration factors other than demand, supply and price will distort the allocation and use of resources in society. Suffice it to say that consideration of the interests of various stakeholders may seem to introduce a tension between the profit motive and the other expectations from a 'for profit' enterprise and has attracted a lot of attention. This is considered in greater detail in Session 3 where corporate social responsibility is discussed. However, you should note that a business supplying a Fairtrade certified product tries to attract customers who endorse fair, ethical and environmentally friendly business practices.

There are other aspects of business decisions where ethical issues arise. For example, investment in environmentally harmful technologies or investment in the regions where human rights violation is suspected may be grounds for questioning business behaviour. Advertising campaigns targeting children may be questioned on ethical grounds. These issues also relate to the stakeholder considerations that you encountered first in Unit 1. In practice, most companies adopt a code of ethics and require their employees to abide by it. Activity 1.2 gives an example of one such code adhered to by a major retailing company in the UK.

Activity 1.2   ....

Marks and Spencer (M&S) Code of Ethics – how we behave

At Marks & Spencer we're committed to doing the right thing for our customers, colleagues, shareholders, suppliers, the environment and our local communities. Our Code of Ethics outlines the behaviours that M&S upholds as a company and expects from you to make sure we conduct business with the highest standards of honesty and integrity. The Code describes key Company policies and procedures and reminds us of behaviours that are unacceptable.

(Marks & Spencer, 2009)

Prepare a list of the stakeholders identified in the extract from the M&S Code of Ethics. (Spend no more than five minutes on this activity.)

Feedback ....

You probably noted customers, employees, shareholders, suppliers, environment and local communities. The extract also mentions that M&S employees must observe high standards of honesty and integrity. You will learn more about ethical principles that accountants are expected to maintain in their behaviour later in this unit. However, at this stage if you want to read the full statement of the M&S Code of Ethics you will find it on the B291 website.

1.2 The need for ethics in accounting

In any enterprise the accounting function is at the centre of what the enterprise communicates to the different stakeholders through its financial statements, hence an accountant needs to be aware of the wider implications of financial reports. This issue is all the more significant in the case of public limited companies. The public limited company form of organisation (as with companies generally) means the separation of ownership and management. In other words, the managers manage and control the business on behalf of its shareholders. This creates a potential conflict of interests between the owners (principals) and the managers (agents). This is called the agency problem, which was explained in Unit 1. This agency problem manifests itself when managers conduct the business in a manner that is not in the best interests of the owners. For example, when managers knowingly take decisions that may improve short-term profits but which may jeopardise the long-term survival of the business, it is referred to as the agency problem. However, as mentioned earlier, owners are not the only stakeholders. There are creditors, customers, employees and potential investors too. One of the main factors responsible for the agency problem is information asymmetry between managers and owners. Independent audit of financial statements by external auditors and transparency in reporting of relevant financial and other information are two of the mechanisms whereby this information asymmetry may be reduced. Various mechanisms to monitor the performance of managers are discussed in greater detail in Session 2 as part of corporate governance frameworks.

In the preceding units you learned that financial statements are prepared in accordance with International Financial Reporting Standards (IFRS) or some other comprehensive basis of accounting. However, there is still scope for judgement on the part of accountants in the process of recording and reporting the financial information. For example, in Unit 3 you learned about the valuation of inventories. Generally, enterprises are expected to follow accounting policies consistently and make changes only when required by changes in situation and/or regulation. Suppose an enterprise changes its inventory valuation method; this could result in a material impact on the reported profit, perhaps by showing an increase in profits. Further suppose that payment of bonuses to the management is related to reported profits. Such a compensation scheme creates incentives for executives to manage earnings through changes in accounting policies.

Therefore, it is important that the accounting treatment of various assets, liabilities, revenues and expenses is done in a way that not only complies with accounting principles and regulations but also represents a 'true and fair' view of the financial condition of the business.

The meaning of a true and fair view is discussed in Session 4 of this unit.

Many situations arise in business where accountants may be called upon to judge the appropriateness of particular actions. Activity 1.3 describes a fictitious accountant's dilemma.

1.3 Approaches to ethics in accounting

Individuals working in organisations have to resolve the ethical dilemmas faced by business enterprises. There may or may not be an ethical code of conduct within an organisation. Even though public limited companies are expected to comply with some form of corporate governance code, these are not necessarily the same as an ethical code. In many business situations unethical practices (such as bribery) are easily dealt with if they are illegal in a country where the enterprise operates, so managers need do nothing other than follow the law. However, consider the situation described in Activity 1.3 and reflect on whether the course of action that the accountant takes is ethical or unethical.

Activity 1.3 ....

P. Ting is a professionally qualified accountant and works as senior accountant for Alpha-Zeta Ltd. The finance director of the company has complete trust in Mr Ting and usually agrees with Mr Ting's interpretation of accounting issues. A recently recruited business development manager in the company claimed some 'miscellaneous' expenses as part of his marketing trip expenses. On enquiring of the manager, Mr Ting found that those miscellaneous expenses actually represented the cost of expensive gifts that were given to an employee of a government department who could potentially give some contracts to Alpha-Zeta. Mr Ting knows that company policy prohibits payment of bribes in cash or kind in expectation of generating business for the company. On Mr Ting's questioning the legitimacy of this expense, the business development manager said that to ensure that contracts were given to Alpha-Zeta he had no choice but to give gifts, as he knew that a competing firm's representative had obtained orders by following this practice. Mr Ting could record this as an expense and be sure that the finance director would accept the payment if he recommended it. He is also aware that any potential benefits from the contract would be significant for the company. Mr Ting considered two alternative courses of action:

(a) report this as a violation of company ethics policy to the finance director and do not approve the expenses

(b) approve this expense as a business development expense on the grounds that the business development manager was newly recruited and perhaps did not fully understand the ethical standards followed by Alpha-Zeta.

The consequences of option (a) are a possible disciplinary action against the business development manager and the loss of potential future business.

The consequences of option (b) are setting a precedent for unethical practices and potential financial gains for the business.

Write down which course of action you would recommend to Mr Ting, giving reasons for your recommendation. (Spend no more than 20 minutes on this activity.)

Feedback

Approaching the situation purely from a compliance perspective you would have, perhaps, recommended option (a) based on the arguments that approving such practice violates company policy and also sets an undesirable precedent for the future. However, considering that the manager is new and that, perhaps, he had failed to digest fully the company's ethical values, you might have opted for (b) as an exception. In the following paragraphs you will find a principles-based framework that may help in these situations. You could argue that Mr Ting should discuss the problem with the finance director or pass on the issue for resolution by the finance director.

"And so the Little Corporate Raider grew to understand that 'unethical' was not the same as 'illegal,' and he lived happily ever after. The end."

1.3.1   The Code of Ethics for accountants

As Activity 1.3 shows, accountants can and do face ethical dilemmas that require resolution. The professional accounting bodies and higher education institutions try to prepare future accountants to deal with these dilemmas. The International Ethics Standards Board for Accountants (IESBA) is an independent standard-setting body that develops an internationally appropriate *Code of Ethics for Professional Accountants*. IESBA can be found via the website of the International Federation of Accountants (IFAC), which is a global organisation of accounting professionals and professional bodies. Most professional accounting bodies in the UK and other countries are members of IFAC and, therefore, the IESBA code of ethics is relevant for practically all professional accountants whether they work in public practice or in business. The following box contains an explanation of the difference between a professional accountant in business and one in public practice.

Difference between a professional accountant in public practice and one in business

A professional accountant in business is employed or engaged in an executive or non-executive capacity in areas such as commerce, industry, service, the public sector, education, the not-for-profit sector, regulatory bodies or professional bodies, or a professional accountant contracted by such entities.

A professional accountant in business may be a salaried employee, a partner, a director (whether executive or non-executive), an owner/manager, a volunteer, or another working for one or more employing organisations. The legal form of the relationship with the employing organisation, if any, has no bearing on the ethical responsibilities incumbent on the professional accountant in business.

A professional accountant in public practice is a professional accountant, irrespective of functional classification (e.g., audit, tax or consulting), in a firm that provides professional services. This term is also used to refer to a firm of professional accountants in public practice.

Professional services: Services requiring accountancy or related skills performed by a professional accountant including accounting, auditing, taxation, management consulting and financial management services.

Source: Adapted from the *Members' Handbook* (Institute of Chartered Accountants in England and Wales, 2009, p. 285)

Fundamental principles of professional and ethical conduct for accountants suggest that accountants' responsibility goes further than serving their own interests or the interests of the organisation for which they work. Most codes of ethics for professional accountants suggest that accounting and audit practices should be in the public interest. The IESBA code of ethics requires that accountants should discharge their duties in the public interest. Public interest could be interpreted as something that would benefit community as a whole.

Responsibility of professional accountants:

A distinguishing mark of the accountancy profession is its acceptance of the responsibility to act in the public interest. Therefore, a professional accountant's responsibility is not exclusively to satisfy the needs of an individual client or employer. In acting in the public interest, a professional accountant shall observe and comply with this Code. If a professional accountant is prohibited from complying with certain parts of this Code by law or regulation, the professional accountant shall comply with all other parts of this Code.

Figure 1 Responsibility of professional accountants
Source: Adapted from p. 6 of the *Code of Ethics for Professional Accountants* (IFAC, 2009).

Most international professional accounting bodies have adopted codes of ethics that broadly correspond to the following fundamental ethical principles recommended by IESBA (2012, Section 100.5).

(a) *Integrity*: a professional accountant should be straightforward and honest in all professional and business relationships.

(b) *Objectivity*: a professional accountant should not allow bias, conflict of interest or undue influence of others to override professional or business judgements.

(c) *Professional competence and due care*: a professional accountant has a continuing duty to maintain professional knowledge and skill at the level required to ensure that a client or employer receives competent professional service based on current developments in practice, legislation and techniques. A professional accountant should act diligently and in accordance with applicable technical and professional standards when providing professional services.

(d) *Confidentiality*: a professional accountant should respect the confidentiality of information acquired as a result of professional and business relationships and should not disclose any such information to third parties without proper and specific authority unless there is a legal or professional right or duty to disclose. Confidential information acquired as a result of professional and business relationships should not be used for the personal advantage of either the professional accountant or third parties.

(e) *Professional behaviour*: a professional accountant should comply with relevant laws and regulations and should avoid any action that discredits the profession.

Activity 1.4

Visit the websites of professional accounting bodies such as ACCA (www.accaglobal.com), CIMA (www.cimaglobal.com), ICAEW (www.icaew.com) and familiarise yourself with their codes of ethics. (Spend no more than 30 minutes on this activity.)

Feedback

You may have noted that all three professional accounting bodies have codes of ethics similar in content and approach to the IFAC code of ethics discussed in this unit.

1.3.2 A conceptual framework to deal with ethical dilemmas

The five fundamental principles of ethical behaviour by which accountants must abide were outlined above. However, this knowledge of fundamental principles is not enough. It was mentioned earlier that accountants have a professional responsibility to perform their duties in the public interest and not to compromise fundamental principles. If, in certain countries, laws require a judgement that is not in accordance with fundamental principles, then the law of the land supersedes the fundamental principles. In all other situations, when faced with an ethical dilemma professional accountants should ensure that the five fundamental principles are not compromised.

The conceptual framework for dealing with ethical dilemmas, as recommended by IFAC and most professional accounting bodies, involves the following six step systematic approach.

Step 1   Identifying and understanding the relevant facts.

Step 2   Identifying the ethical issues involved.

Step 3   Identifying which fundamental principles are threatened in the matter in question.

Step 4   Considering the established internal procedures.

Step 5   Evaluating alternative courses of action.

Step 6   Choosing an appropriate course of action.

Step 1 simply means to become familiar with the facts of the situation and understand the issues. The next step is to identify the ethical issues involved. When the situation involved requires a decision that might compromise any of the fundamental principles then it is worth considering what the threats are to fundamental principles. To identify threats to any fundamental principles, an accountant should be aware of possible threats in different circumstances to his/her integrity and independence of judgement. For example, if an accountant is on an auditing engagement, and one of the senior executives of the company whose accounts he is auditing has been a close friend for a long time, this situation may create what is known as a familiarity threat. The five threats listed by IFAC are described below (adapted from IFAC (2005, pp. 8–9)).

- *Self-interest*: when a financial or other interest will inappropriately influence the professional accountant's judgement, compromising his/her objectivity or integrity for example.

- *Self-review*: when a previous judgement needs to be re-evaluated by the professional accountant responsible for that judgement.

- *Advocacy*: when a professional accountant promotes a position or opinion to the point that subsequent objectivity may be compromised.

- *Familiarity*: when, because of a close relationship, a professional accountant becomes too sympathetic to the interests of others (as described above).

- *Intimidation*: when a professional accountant may be deterred from acting objectively by threats, actual or perceived.

The Auditing Practices Board (APB) mentions management threat as an additional threat to the objectivity and independence of the auditor. The Auditing Practices Board defines management threat as a threat that exists 'when the audit firm undertakes work that involves making judgments and taking decisions that are properly the responsibility of management' (APB, 2008, p. 10).

When a professional accountant identifies any threat in a given situation, he/she should evaluate the significance of the threat by considering the substance and materiality of the issue. If the threat can be eliminated or reduced by taking particular action, then this should be suggested by the professional accountant. If the threat cannot be eliminated, the professional accountant should raise the issue with relevant people in the organisation. A professional accountant should be prepared to disassociate himself/herself from a course of action that would violate professional ethical principles. In extreme situations this may involve a decision to resign from the audit engagement or from the firm. The box below contains a description of an ethical dilemma faced by an accountant followed by an explanation of how to use the conceptual framework to resolve the dilemma.

An accountant's dilemma

Consider a situation where a company's shares are publicly traded and the company is subject to compliance with International Financial Reporting Standards (IFRS). The company carries a large amount of intangible assets (including goodwill and some brands) in its balance sheet. The professionally qualified accountant of the company is in the process of finalising the financial reports for the year. During the process a report on estimated changes to the value of intangible assets is brought to his attention. According to the report, prepared by competent financial and business analysts, the obtainable fair value of intangible assets is much lower than the value presently recorded in the balance sheet of the company. In the accountant's judgement this needs to be reflected in the accounts by writing down the value of intangible assets and recognising the fall in value as an expense in the income statement for the financial period. The effect of this will be a reduction in the profits reported for the year.

The chief executive officer (CEO) is informed by the accountant that the fair obtainable value of the intangible assets is much lower than the book value that the company is carrying and needs to be written down. The chief executive officer does not agree with the accountant. In his view, the estimated changes to the value of intangible assets are very subjective and do not reflect their true potential. The CEO does not want to record any change to the value of intangible assets.

If the accountant does not recognise the expense in the current year, the company will report a higher profit figure than would otherwise be the case for the year. If the accountant insists on recognising the expense, the current year's profits will be reduced and perhaps will affect the accountant's relationship with the CEO.

The International Accounting Standard 36 (IAS) requires that if there is an indication that the value of intangible assets has been impaired during the year, it should be disclosed and recorded appropriately in the financial reports.

Resolving the dilemma

The dilemma could be resolved by applying the conceptual framework in the following way.

Identifying and understanding the relevant facts

There is a difference of opinion on the fair, obtainable value of the intangible assets. According to accounting standards the impairment to the value of intangible assets should be recognised and recorded in the financial reports.

Identifying the ethical issues involved

The ethical issue in the situation is either to keep to the professional and objective judgement or to compromise on it by agreeing with the CEO's viewpoint.

Photo of 'The Thinker' by Auguste Rodin

Identifying which fundamental principles are threatened in the matter in question

According to the estimates of the financial analysts there has been an impairment to the value of the company's intangible assets. If the accountant feels intimidated by the CEO he may agree to the CEO's suggestion. This will lead to a compromise on objectivity and integrity.

Considering the established internal procedures

No detailed information is provided in the example except that the company's shares are publicly traded. This implies that it is listed and will also be audited by an external auditor to ensure compliance with IFRS. If the accountant agrees with the CEO's viewpoint, it will lead to non-compliance with a financial reporting standard (IAS 36) that as a qualified accountant he should follow.

Evaluating alternative courses of action

In this situation the accountant has two options.

1   Agree with the chief executive officer and ignore the impairment losses.

2   Recognise and record the impairment losses.

Option one means the accountant must compromise his objectivity in judgement and do something that will not be consistent with reporting standards.

Option two implies compliance with reporting standards and protecting the accountant's professional judgement and objectivity.

There is, however, the chance that choosing option two may impact on the accountant's relationship with the CEO. As a professional accountant, he needs to evaluate these options and decide on a course of action.

Choosing an appropriate course of action

To protect the fundamental principles and eliminate the threat, the accountant should make his views clear; that is, recognising and recording the impairment losses in the current year will be in line with best accounting practice. However, the accountant should be prepared to face the consequences of not agreeing with the CEO's viewpoint, which may potentially create problems for his employment within the company.

If there is too much pressure to agree with the CEO, it may amount to an intimidation threat, which the accountant could report to the board or disclose to the appropriate regulatory authority. Such **whistle-blowing** is a possible course of action for a professional accountant in extreme cases. In addition, most professional accounting bodies may provide dedicated ethics counselling facilities for their members, which members could use to seek guidance when attempting to resolve ethical dilemmas.

Activity 1.5 ....

Go back to the situation described in Activity 1.3 and revisit the discussion. Using the five principles of ethical behaviour and the framework for dealing with ethical dilemmas, recommend a course of action, giving reasons for your choice. (Spend no more than 25 minutes on this activity.)

Feedback ....

Following the conceptual framework for dealing with ethical dilemmas, you may approach this dilemma by first noting the facts of the situation. The facts are that a new business development manager has incurred expenses on an activity that is against the company's ethics policy. The expenses were incurred with the expectation of future orders. Mr Ting, who is authorised to take a view on this expense, is trusted by his superiors. The ethical issue involved is whether to approve the expense based on the arguments given in the situation. There is a threat to the objectivity and integrity principles. Mr Ting should ascertain whether the new manager was aware of the company's ethics policy (i.e., knew internal procedures). If he was, then Mr Ting cannot be sympathetic and must not approve the expense as it is a clear violation of the company's ethics policy. Objectivity demands that Mr Ting's judgement should not be biased. Fearing to take disciplinary action against the new manager and therefore taking a sympathetic view may compromise Mr Ting's objectivity. Approving this expense also violates the integrity of the company's reporting and may result in Mr Ting losing the confidence of his superiors if they should come to know of this choice.

Summary

In this session you have learned about the meaning of and need for ethics in accounting and business contexts. The discussion here is related to earlier units, particularly Unit 1, where wider implications of accounting practice were discussed. The meaning of ethics originally did not connote anything good or bad but merely common practices and customs. However, in the context of the current debates in the business world the term 'ethics' assumes a connotation of giving consideration to the interests of wider stakeholders in addition to making profits. Recall Singer's view that ethical judgement implies going beyond one's own personal point of view and considering the implications of an action from an impartial perspective for a wider group of stakeholders.

You then learned about the approach to accounting ethics taken by professional accounting bodies. In addition to corporate codes of ethics you learned about the IFAC's code of ethics, which emphasises five ethical principles; namely, integrity, objectivity, professional competence and due care, confidentiality and professional behaviour. An important element of the professional responsibility of accountants is that they should fulfil their duties in the public interest. A conceptual framework to deal with ethical dilemmas was also presented and illustrated. Some of the issues discussed in this session will reappear in Session 4, where you will be learning about fraud prevention and detection. In Session 2 you will learn about the principles of corporate governance, which aim to ensure the accountability of management to various stakeholders and reduce agency problems.

SESSION 2 Corporate governance

Introduction

Upon completion of Session 2 you are expected to:

- understand the context, meaning and development of corporate governance
- understand the main elements of corporate governance
- be able to explain the differences between a principles-based and a rules-based approach to corporate governance.

From the discussion in Session 1 two relationships became apparent. The first was the relationship between an organisation and society in general. For example, Activity 1.1 illustrated the tension between the organisational goal of making profits and society's concern to protect the rights of children. The second was the relationship between the managers and the owners of an organisation. These relationships sometimes create the possibility of conflicting expectations from different stakeholders.

There is also a link between ethical issues and corporate governance issues. For example, unscrupulous conduct by an accountant might damage the reputation of a business enterprise thereby harming the interests of its owners. At the same time it may shake the confidence of suppliers, potential investors and so on. Fraudulent misreporting of financial performance is illegal and once disclosed can lead to serious consequences for the survival of a business entity. Unethical and illegal accounting decisions and reporting were the main causes of the collapse of the US-based major multinational corporation Enron. The bankruptcy of Enron highlighted weak corporate governance mechanisms, which led to poor risk management, and put a question mark against the reliability of financial reports in terms of providing a true and fair record of the financial position of the company.

In this session you will learn what corporate governance is and why the need for it has emerged more strongly in recent years. You will also learn that there are different approaches to corporate governance and differences in what corporate governance codes mean when considered from accounting and auditing perspectives.

2.1 The context and development of corporate governance

In most modern economies, particularly in developed economies, a substantial part of private sector economic activity is controlled by large corporations. Most large publicly traded companies are characterised by the separation of ownership and control of business activities. In proprietorship or partnership firms the owners are usually the managers of the business. They are also the residual claimants of the profits or losses from the business. When partners appoint managers they will generally monitor the performance of those managers closely. Hence, in this type of entity there is no conflict between the interests of the owners and those of the managers.

However, a large publicly traded company may have thousands of owners (shareholders) who do not have direct control over the running of the corporate entity owned by them. The control of the business lies in the hands of a board of directors who are appointed by the shareholders. This results in what is called the principal–agent relationship where owners are the principals and managers are the agents (see also Section 1.2). Another feature of public limited companies is the changing ownership pattern of companies. Suppose a company is owned by thousands of shareholders each owning only a small number of shares. It is quite common for such shareholders to hold their shares only for a short time before selling them. Most of the time, individual shareholders with few shares do not have the time and/or sufficient financial skills to analyse carefully the performance of the company. In such a situation small individual investors are not in a position to monitor the performance of the executives of the company. When a company's shares are owned by institutional investors or individual investors with large shareholdings, one may argue that these types of investor are more interested in monitoring the performance of the executives. They will also be in a better position to collect and analyse the information about the company's performance. However, institutional investors may also sell their shares.

Thus, the changing and, in many cases, diffused ownership structure of companies may weaken the incentive of shareholders to monitor the performance of managers. A point worth noting is that the ownership pattern of companies is not the same in all countries. In the UK and the USA, where companies are financed mainly through stock markets, the pattern of ownership may change as described above. However, there are other financing models where banks play a bigger role in financing companies, such as in Japan and Germany. In such a situation the banks and other such institutional investors would monitor the performance of the executives. The general point is that not all types of owner have the same level of interest in monitoring a company's performance because of differences in the amounts they have invested, their investment periods, access to information and the ability to analyse the performance of the executives of large companies.

The word 'control' refers to those controlling a firm, that is, the managers.

The executives in control of operations typically are much better informed about the company's business situation than the shareholders. This raises the issue of potential conflicts of interest. Typically, shareholders expect the executives to manage the company's operations to increase the profits and thereby increase the share price. However, because managers may have relatively more information about the business and more control over the business they may not pursue the objective of increasing the profits as much as they would if they were also the owners of the business. Theorists call this the agency problem.

The foregoing features of public limited companies and the implications of agency relationships are used as arguments that the managers of large corporations need to be accountable to different stakeholders in business. The debate about the conflicting interests of managers and shareholders is not new. In the 1930s, for instance, this issue was raised by Berle and Means (1933) in their book *The Modern Corporation and Private Property*, when they argued that the separation of owners from control of the organisation created a situation where managers enjoyed far too much power and pursued their own interests rather than those of the owners. Berle and Means argued that the profit incentives that motivate the owners of small enterprises may not be sufficient motivation for managers since, as they are paid executives, managers' motivations could be focused on issues other than profits. Berle and Means appear to allude to other motives that managers may pursue, such as building empires:

> Just what motives are effective today, in so far as control is concerned, must be a matter of conjecture. But it is probable that more could be learned regarding them by studying the motives of an Alexander the Great, seeking new worlds to conquer, than by considering the motives of a petty tradesman of the days of Adam Smith.
>
> (Berle and Means, 1933, p. 350)

This divergence in the interests of managers and those of owners is at the heart of the debate on corporate governance and was noted well before Berle and Means, by the father of economics, Adam Smith, who also remained sceptical about the ability and intentions of managers (board directors) of large companies. There were few large joint stock companies in existence in the latter half of the eighteenth century when Adam Smith's book *An Inquiry into the Nature and Causes of the Wealth of Nations* (often referred to by the short title *The Wealth of Nations*) was published in 1776. These large companies mostly dealt in foreign trade, shipping and other such businesses. Even with such a limited number of companies to observe, Adam Smith's comments presaged the agency problem some 200 years before it was formally articulated by Jensen and Meckling (1976).

Smith's use of 'court' can be considered as being the equivalent to 'board of directors' and 'private copartnery' can be understood as a partnership.

The trade of a joint stock company is always managed by a court of directors. This court, indeed, is frequently subject, in many respects, to the control of a general court of proprietors. But the greater part of those proprietors seldom pretend to understand anything of the business of the company, and when the spirit of action happens not to prevail among them, give themselves no trouble about it, but receive contentedly such half-yearly or yearly dividend as the directors think proper to make to them. This total exemption from trouble and from risk, beyond a limited sum, encourages many people to become adventurers in joint stock companies, who would, upon no account, hazard their fortunes in any private copartnery. ...The directors of such companies, however, being the managers rather of other people's money than of their own, it cannot well be expected that they should watch over it with the same anxious vigilance with which the partners in a private copartnery frequently watch over their own. Like the stewards of a rich man, they are apt to consider attention to small matters as not for their master's honour, and very easily give themselves a dispensation from having it. Negligence and profusion, therefore, must always prevail, more or less, in the management of the affairs of such a company.

(Smith, 1776, pp. 989–900)

Smith's remarks also point to individual investors' lack of understanding about the complexity of the businesses in which they invest as shareholders and also their inability to exercise effective control over the management. This is particularly relevant in today's context where large companies operate in different countries and engage in a variety of businesses where the ownership structure could be very diverse, ranging from individual shareholders to large pension funds, institutions and private equity funds. This situation is further compounded by the fact that modern corporations are expected to balance the interests not only of the owners and managers but also of other stakeholders such as consumers, suppliers, environmental groups and so on. The ownership and regulatory complexity of modern businesses have led to a demand for a more structured approach to corporate governance.

Corporate governance is a set of mechanisms that aims to minimise agency problems and ensure that companies do not engage in practices that may be detrimental to the interests of the various stakeholders. Broadly, the corporate governance system in the UK comprises the statutory provisions in the *Companies Act 2006, the Combined Code on Corporate Governance* (2008) (now *The UK Corporate Governance Code* (2010)) issued by the Financial Reporting Council in the UK, and relevant regulations of the London Stock Exchange whereby the interests of the stakeholders in companies are protected. In the case of banking and other financial companies, the additional legislation in the *Financial Services and Markets Act 2000* provides a framework for monitoring by Financial Services Authority.

Unit 6 will often refer to the 'UK Combined Code' and you should take this to mean the 2010 version mentioned here, unless told otherwise.

Corporate governance closely relates to the major purposes of accounting and auditing. For example, in Unit 1 we discussed the point that financial reports are used by different stakeholders to form a judgement about the performance of a firm. To ensure that a firm meets the expectations of different stakeholders, there should be adequate mechanisms in place to ensure that senior managers and board members fulfil their fiduciary duties. There have been increasing calls to put some systems and procedures in place, which lay down specific requirements on disclosure and the constitution of boards, set out rules to link the performance of the board with remuneration policies, and also deal with risk management and internal audit. This need has arisen from two main reasons:

1   *Accountability of management.* As was indicated above, there is a need for management to manage a business in the interests of owners and other stakeholders with integrity and due care, while aiming to minimise the risk of any losses and possible bankruptcy. Various mechanisms of corporate governance have, therefore, evolved to ensure that management performs and accounts for its roles effectively.

2   *International movement of funds.* Increasing globalisation of financial markets has meant that shareholders and lenders are investing in companies outside their domestic markets. The financial reports therefore need to be prepared in such a way that

they can be understood by suppliers of funds from different countries. This is most clearly reflected in the development of International Financial Reporting Standards (IFRS). Underpinning this development is the need for transparency and uniformity in disclosure practices to enable proper scrutiny by the users of financial reports.

As a result of several high profile corporate scandals, such as Enron and WorldCom, major steps have been taken by governments and professional bodies to strengthen the oversight of company performance by external agencies such as the Securities and Exchange Commission (SEC) in the USA. The USA also passed legislation called the *Sarbanes–Oxley Act (SOX)* in 2002. This Act requires all companies listed on the New York Stock Exchange to be transparent and follow various rules. The rules relate to the creation of various committees at board level to manage risks and to ensure adequacy of internal controls, among other things. In the UK, since the early 1990s, similar corporate governance systems have evolved, starting with the Cadbury Committee's report in 1992 (known as the 'Cadbury Report'; full title: *The Financial Aspects of Corporate Governance*) which proposed best practices for corporate board structures. Many member countries of the Organisation of Economic Cooperation and Development (OECD), a group of 31 rich countries, also produced their own country-specific corporate governance codes. There is a private voluntary body sponsored by several professional accounting bodies, called the Committee of Sponsoring Organisations of the Treadway Commission (COSO), which provides guidance on corporate governance and business ethics based on the research it carries out on corporate reporting and business practices. Here, though, we focus on the development of the UK corporate governance systems and their implications in the context of accounting and auditing, but note that the issues addressed by different country-specific governance codes are in fact quite similar.

In the UK, the Cadbury Committee (1992) was followed by the Greenbury Committee (1995), which examined and recommended best practices for directors' remuneration. This was followed by several other reports and has resulted in the publication of *The UK Corporate Governance Code* (2010). Governance systems in companies have thus evolved over time in the UK in response to a series of reports on different aspects of governance in public limited companies, which have covered the roles of chairman, board of directors, risk and audit committees, non-executive directors, and executive remuneration, among other issues. Similarly, in many countries around the world there have been various developments in corporate governance. However, the essential features of all governance codes are to provide the ways and means for regulators, investors and other stakeholders to ensure that firms use their resources in the best interests of their stakeholders.

Activity 2.1   ....

Visit the website of the European Corporate Governance Institute, via the link on the B291 website, and find the Combined Code of the UK and any other country in which you may be interested. Try to find three similarities and/or three differences between the UK Combined Code and that of the other country code chosen by you. (Spend no more than 35 minutes on this activity.)

There is no feedback for this activity, but it may be a good idea to use the forums on the B291 website to share the similarities and differences you find.

2.2 The meaning and objectives of corporate governance

The Cadbury Report (1992) provided a definition and context of corporate governance code in the UK as:

> the system by which companies are directed and controlled. Boards of directors are responsible for the governance of their companies. The shareholders' role in governance is to appoint the directors and the auditors and to satisfy themselves that an appropriate governance structure is in place. The responsibilities of the board include setting the company's strategic aims, providing the leadership to put them into effect, supervising the management of the business and reporting to shareholders on their stewardship. The board's actions are subject to laws, regulations and the shareholders in general meeting.
>
> (Cadbury Committee, 1992)

The Combined Code (2008) reinforced this shareholder-centric view in that the preamble (p. 1) to the Code says that good corporate governance 'should contribute to better performance by helping a board discharge its duties in the interests of shareholders; if it is ignored, the consequences may well be vulnerability or poor performance. Good governance should facilitate efficient, effective and entrepreneurial management that can deliver shareholder value over the longer term'.

The banking crisis in 2008–09 triggered not only the reappraisal of governance systems for banking and financial companies, but also resulted in a review of the Combined Code by Financial Reporting Council (FRC). Sir David Walker, who reviewed corporate governance arrangements for banking and financial companies in the UK, defines the role of corporate governance as 'to protect and advance the interests of shareholders through setting the strategic direction of a company and appointing and monitoring capable management to achieve this' (Walker, 2009, p. 23). The UK corporate governance has also been updated to reflect the changes in the expectations of the governance code in the light of financial crisis. The Combined Code, which is applicable to all publicly traded companies listed on the London Stock Exchange, describes 'the purpose of the corporate governance to facilitate effective, entrepreneurial and prudent management that can deliver the long-term success of the company' (*The UK Corporate Governance Code*, 2010, p. 1).

According to these definitions, the primary stakeholders in UK companies are assumed to be shareholders. An alternative view is from a stakeholder perspective, which considers that an organisation is part of wider society and therefore its performance and impact concern a wider set of stakeholders. This is reflected in the following definition of corporate governance:

> Corporate governance involves a set of relationships between a company's management, its board, its shareholders and other stakeholders. Corporate governance also provides the structure through which the objectives of the company are set, and the means of attaining those objectives and monitoring performance are determined.
>
> (OECD, 2004, p. 11)

Both definitions indicate that corporate governance mechanisms comprise a set of good practices that aims to ensure effective accountability of the management to the shareholders and other stakeholders. The main difference between the UK Combined Code and the OECD definition is the stronger focus on shareholder value maximisation in the former, although it is worth noting here that the principal stakeholders may include not only shareholders but also lenders of large amounts of money, such as bankers and government.

Considering the above definitions, the scope of corporate governance can be said to include the following three aspects of corporate governance:

- objectives of corporate governance
- stakeholder relations
- requirement of structure and processes.

Objectives and processes are discussed in the following section and stakeholder relations are discussed in more detail in Session 3. However, before that, please attempt Activity 2.2 to clarify your understanding of stakeholders.

Activity 2.2

Write down a few thoughts on how the government of a country could be a key stakeholder in a 100 per cent privately owned large bank. (Spend about five to ten minutes on this activity.)

Feedback

An interesting example of the government as a stakeholder in private banks was witnessed in the aftermath of the financial and banking crisis that occurred during 2007–08. Several large multinational banks in the UK, the USA and many other countries were faced with serious threats to their solvency during 2007–08. Many governments stepped in to strengthen the financial position of banks and other financial institutions by providing huge loans. In some cases, such as the Northern Rock bank in the UK, institutions were, in effect, nationalised. In cases such as these, even though the government was not a direct stakeholder as an owner or an investor in these banks, it decided to commit public finances to rescue many of them. The argument put forward for this decision was that financial institutions and banks were so integral to the economy that the government could not just let the banks fail.

The banking crisis of 2007–08 also raised many issues relating to corporate governance in the finance industry, and forced the government in the UK to review corporate governance mechanisms in finance and banking companies. The main issues covered by this review included:

- the effectiveness of risk management at board level, including the incentives provided by remuneration policy to manage risk effectively
- the balance of skills, experience and independence required on the boards of UK banking institutions
- the effectiveness of board practices and the performance of audit, risk, remuneration and nomination committees
- the role of institutional shareholders in engaging effectively with companies and monitoring boards.

Corporate governance mechanisms aim to achieve the following objectives:

- to ensure transparency and reliability in the reporting of relevant information for various stakeholders in an entity
- to ensure there are systems in place in the organisational structure and management that make an organisation and its management accountable for performance with respect to organisational goals.

To achieve these two broad objectives, a good corporate governance system would pursue the following specific aims:

1 *Achievement of strategic objectives.* Every organisation has a set of strategic objectives. An effective corporate governance system should ensure that these strategic objectives are achieved.

2 *Minimise and mitigate risks.* Organisations face legal, financial, reputational and business risks. As part of effective corporate governance requirements, procedures and processes are needed to identify, mitigate and manage different risks. For example, a risk committee for a large chemical manufacturing company may assess the adequacy of the risk identification procedures, risk management procedures and to what extent risk management is embedded into the day to day management culture of the company.

3 *Fulfil responsibilities to stakeholders.* An effective corporate governance requirement will be that there are systems in place in the organisation whereby conflicting interests of different stakeholders, if any, are discussed and dealt with fairly and transparently.

4 *Independence of non-executive (independent) directors, internal and external auditors.* Non-executive directors are expected to play a vital role in the effectiveness of corporate governance as they are expected to provide internal oversight and monitoring of the behaviour of executive directors and senior management of the company. Therefore, ensuring the independence of non-executive directors is a key objective of an effective corporate governance system. Similarly, internal and external auditors need to be independent to be able to provide objective and impartial assessment and reports. An effective corporate governance system will ensure that their independence is secured.

5 *Clear statement of accountability.* An effective corporate governance system will aim to ensure that the responsibilities and accountability of the senior management are clearly established.

6 *Timely, relevant and reliable data.* For any group or committee involved at senior management level and other stakeholders, such as owners, timely availability of relevant and reliable data, financial and non-financial reports is crucial to the effectiveness of decision making. Most corporate governance codes lay down detailed requirements and also specify different roles that should be identified as part of the corporate governance system. Governance codes thus deal with the roles and responsibilities of the board of directors, senior management and those of auditors.

There are broadly two approaches to specifying these roles and responsibilities. They are generally known as the principles-based approach to corporate governance and the rules-based approach to corporate governance. Under the principles-based approach, the main principles of corporate governance are set out and organisations are expected to comply with them or to explain, if they do not comply, why they do not. This 'comply or explain' principle is distinct from a rules-based approach where the management of the company is required to follow the rules of corporate governance. Under the rules-based approach good governance principles are prescribed and the management of companies is required by law to follow the rules and regulations.

The UK Combined Code is an example of the principles-based approach. All big companies listed on the London Stock Exchange (usually the top 350 companies) are required to comply with the principles enshrined in the UK Combined Code or explain wherever they do not comply.

The USA's *Sarbanes–Oxley Act 2002* is an example of the rules-based approach. The Securities and Exchange Commission in the USA is empowered to ensure that companies listed on the New York Stock Exchange abide by the requirements of the *Sarbanes–Oxley Act*. However, in Section 2.3 we will be focusing more on the principles-based system as illustrated by the UK's Combined Code. It is also worth noting that the 'principles as opposed to rules' framework is one way to understand and classify the different corporate governance systems found in different countries. Another way of classifying the corporate governance systems is according to the primacy of stakeholder claims assumed by companies. For example, in companies in the UK and the USA, where capital markets are the main providers of capital, the shareholders are considered primary stakeholders. However, in countries such as Germany, Japan and France, the stakeholder view is more widespread in corporate governance systems. You will see some examples of these differences in Section 2.3.

2.3 Key elements of corporate governance in the UK

We mentioned earlier that approaches towards corporate governance vary depending on the country in which the business is located. Thus it is not easy to explain in detail about corporate governance in an international context. For example, we noted earlier that there is a big difference in the way that US and UK corporate governance is practised. Similarly, corporate governance in Germany, France and Japan also varies because of the distinctive features of corporate management structures found in these countries. Therefore, for the purpose of illustrating a framework of corporate governance, we will discuss the corporate governance framework based on the UK's Combined Code.

The key elements of corporate governance rules in the UK revolve around the following aspects of company management:

- board of directors
- remuneration of directors and senior managers
- accountability and audit
- relations with shareholders and institutional shareholders.

2.3.1 Board of directors

The board of directors provides the leadership and strategic management of a company. It is expected that the board will use all the resources at its disposal effectively and efficiently to achieve corporate objectives. The board is usually headed by a chairperson and comprises a chief executive officer, executive directors and non-executive directors. They are collectively responsible for the performance of the company.

The provisions of the UK Combined Code recommend that the chairperson and the chief executive should not be the same person and that there should be a clear division of responsibilities between the chairperson and the chief executive. The chairperson is responsible for providing leadership to the board and ensuring that the board fulfils its responsibilities. The role of the chairperson therefore includes setting the agenda for the board and ensuring that directors receive appropriate, accurate, timely and clear information. The chairperson should also ensure effective representation of the non-executive directors and contribution by them to good management of the company. The chairperson is expected to be independent of the executive team and is responsible for effective communication with the shareholders. The role of the chief executive is not clearly spelt out in the Combined Code, and perhaps rightly so as it is the board of directors led by the chairperson who would be in a better position to articulate the role of chief executive – by considering the strategic objectives and mission of the company. However, the chief executive will usually lead on formulation and implementation of a company's strategies. In this role he/she will usually be seen as a key executive, accountable to the board of the company and other stakeholders.

The directors are appointed to the board through a transparent and formal procedure based on objective criteria and merit. For this purpose the Code provides that there should be a Nominations Committee of the board, chaired by an independent (non-executive) director, who recommends people with suitable skills and the knowledge required to meet the objectives of the company.

The non-executive directors are not involved in the day to day management of the business but are expected to play a vital part in ensuring the accountability of the executive directors towards shareholders. The Code lists several criteria to be considered when determining the independence of a director, such as past employment within the company, any business relationship with the company, family ties with any of the advisers, directors or senior employees, representing a significant shareholder, and the length of time served on the board. The guiding principle is to check for the factors that could result in a violation of the independence of the directors.

2.3.2 Remuneration of directors and senior managers

Remuneration of directors and senior managers is a key part of the governance mechanism, as it is through remuneration packages that companies attract, appoint and retain good executives. This has also been the most contentious element of corporate governance in practice. The UK Combined Code recommends that a 'significant proportion of executive directors' remuneration should be structured so as to link rewards to corporate and individual performance' (2010, p. 22). While it seems a sound and sensible principle, in practice determining the basis of performance-related remuneration is a difficult task. The guiding principles are transparency and adherence to the formal procedures that the remuneration committee, comprising non-executive directors only, should use.

In practice, the remuneration committee may use the advisory services of expert remuneration consultants for fixing the remuneration of executive directors and other senior managers of the company. Often the remuneration package of senior executives is linked to identifiable performance benchmarks. These performance benchmarks could be target returns to shareholders, profitability, average annual increase in earnings per share over a few years or the increase in the share price relative to some share index. In other words, the performance targets are based on parameters the remuneration committee deems appropriate to ensure that the achievement of agreed targets will be in the interests of shareholders over the long term.

Usually the remuneration of executive directors and senior managers will have three components: fixed annual salary, cash annual bonuses and executive share options. Annual salary is generally the smallest proportion of the total remuneration. Cash bonuses and share options are related to the achievement of agreed targets. Share options allow executives to buy shares in the company for an agreed price, usually with a condition restricting them from selling the shares for a fixed time period. The remuneration committee must also consider other terms and conditions related to the compensation

Earnings per share (EPS) means profit after tax is divided by the total number of ordinary shares issued by a company. (The calculation of EPS is not always straight forward.)

Trends in EPS are monitored by investors and analysts as indicators of financial performance of companies.

packages of executive directors. These may include termination benefits and pension contributions. After the banking and financial crisis of 2007–08, executive bonuses came under close scrutiny and severe criticism for encouraging a culture of excessive risk-taking that jeopardised the whole financial system. Subsequently, there have been demands for more regulation of executive compensation packages and an enhanced role for remuneration committees to balance the interests of shareholders with the need to retain and compensate good executives.

The remuneration of non-executive directors is determined by executive directors and does not usually include share options. The remuneration of non-executive directors should reflect the time they commit to their role on the board.

2.3.3   Accountability and audit

The board of directors is responsible for the achievement of the strategic objectives of the company. Accountability of the board to various stakeholders, therefore, is a key element of corporate governance. The UK Combined Code provisions mention three main principles in this regard: financial and business reporting, risk management and internal control, and accountability and audit. These are discussed below.

The UK Combined Code mentions that 'the board should present a balanced and understandable assessment of the company's position and prospects' (2010, p. 18). This principle implies that the board should put forward a periodic review of the company's performance and its assessment about the risks and opportunities that the business may face over the next few years. This is usually done by the board through the interim reports and annual reports of the company. In the case of exceptional risks, the board may issue a statement to all or specific groups of stakeholders as and when necessary. The UK Combined Code requires that there should be a system of effective internal control to safeguard shareholders' investments and the company's assets.

The board should periodically, and at least once in a year, review the effectiveness of the company's internal controls and should report to the shareholders that it has done so. Internal control systems include financial, operational, compliance and risk management systems. In large companies there could be separate committees for internal control and risk to ensure that a company has effective internal control systems. The committee's report may be published as part of the annual report.

The UK Combined Code's third principle of accountability and audit requires that a company should have formal mechanisms to ensure that the principles of financial reporting and internal control are applied properly. For this, an audit committee comprising at least three independent directors should be established. The main role of an audit committee is to:

- monitor the integrity of the financial statements of the company
- review and assess the effectiveness of the internal control systems

- review and monitor the external auditor's independence and objectivity and the effectiveness of the audit process
- make recommendations regarding the appointment, re-appointment, removal, remuneration and terms of engagement of the external auditor. The board has to put these items for approval before shareholders in a general meeting.

Financial and business reporting, risk management and internal controls, and the role of the audit committee, together create a set of effective corporate governance practices that increase the accountability of the board to shareholders and other stakeholders. A detailed description and discussion of internal controls and audit is provided in Session 4.

2.3.4 Relations with shareholders and institutional shareholders

Enhancing the engagement of shareholders with management is one of the main ways to bridge the communication gap between management and shareholders. The Combined Code puts emphasis on dialogue between the shareholders and the board for the purpose of a mutual understanding of corporate objectives. The board is responsible for ensuring that a satisfactory dialogue with shareholders takes place. Annual general meetings (AGMs) are one of the ways to facilitate this dialogue. However, the board of directors may also inform, consult and seek approval in cases that are too urgent or too important to be left for annual general meetings. This could be done by writing to shareholders, calling general meetings (formerly extraordinary general meetings), or organising postal voting for certain special resolutions. Most governance codes require the chairman of the board of directors to be responsible for ensuring effective communication with the shareholders. This is done by inviting and encouraging shareholders to attend AGMs and ensuring that all directors and chairmen of the audit, remuneration and nominations committees are available to respond to shareholder questions at AGMs.

Institutional investors own a substantial proportion of shares in most public companies. Institutional investors are entities that invest on behalf of their members, such as pensioners (in pension funds), and thus have relatively more competence and resources to evaluate the performance of the board. This makes institutional investors key participants in the governance of many listed companies. The UK Combined Code suggests that institutional shareholders should evaluate the corporate governance mechanisms of the companies in which they invest and apply due pressure to ensure compliance with the best practice in corporate governance. For example, institutional investors could vote against changes to the board structure if these are thought likely to weaken the governance structure of a company.

In summary, principles-based corporate governance does not impose legal requirements on companies but expects voluntary compliance with sound corporate governance practices. However, compliance becomes mandatory if any company chooses to list its shares on a stock exchange as the stock exchange usually requires compliance with the governance code as part of its listing conditions.

As mentioned in Unit 1, the term 'listing' means registering a company with a stock exchange so that the company's shares and other securities can be traded on that stock exchange. The London Stock Exchange requires that all companies listed on the exchange should comply with the UK Combined Code. Thus compliance with the Combined Code, though not a legal requirement, becomes obligatory for companies listing their shares on the London Stock Exchange. The Combined Code provides a framework for the management of companies to disclose in a transparent manner details about performance, accountability and risk management.

Activity 2.3

The UK Combined Code requires that the roles of the chief executive and the chairperson should not be performed by the same individual. However, in 2008–09 Marks & Spencer combined the roles of the chief executive officer and the chairperson – in violation of the recommendation of the UK Combined Code. In April 2008, the then-chairman of Marks and Spencer wrote a letter explaining this departure from compliance with the Combined Code. The chairman offered two main explanations to justify the company's deviation from the Combined Code. First, he argued that it was a temporary arrangement to manage and complete the on-going restructuring of senior management; second, that it was in order to cope with external challenges arising from difficult market conditions following the 2007–08 economic recession.

Read the extracts from the letter (see box below). Then comment on the various changes the company made to its board structure to counterbalance the power vested in the combined post of chief executive and chairman. Do you think these changes would satisfy shareholders and institutional investors?

If you wish, you can read the whole letter (available on the B291 website) but it is not necessary for this activity: just reflect on the foregoing discussion about the board of directors and respond to the question. (Spend no more than 15 minutes on this activity.)

Extract from the letter to Marks & Spencer's shareholders explaining the appointment of a Chief Executive Officer-cum-Chairman

The Board is very conscious of the governance arguments (set out in the Combined Code) that companies should split the roles of Chairman and Chief Executive as it is undesirable to have too much concentration of authority in one person.

However, in deciding to appoint Stuart Rose as Executive Chairman, the Board was aware of the need to put in place balancing controls to mitigate the governance concerns that such a structure might otherwise engender. Accordingly, the Board has agreed the following:

a) **Limited period of appointment until July 2011** when the Company will revert to the conventional model of Chairman and Chief Executive.

b) **Appointment of Sir David Michels as Deputy Chairman** (and continuing his role as Senior Independent Director). Sir David is an experienced and notably independent-minded businessman with considerable knowledge of consumer businesses from his distinguished career in the hospitality business, latterly as Chief Executive of Hilton International. He has also served as a Non-Executive Director on the Boards of a number of UK listed companies. He has committed to spend sufficient and significant time in his role as Deputy Chairman and is resigning from the Boards of The British Land Company PLC and RAB Capital PLC in order to ensure that he can fulfil this commitment.

c) **Clear specification of duties of Executive Chairman and Deputy Chairman** to ensure proper division of responsibilities and balance of power. The Deputy Chairman will have joint responsibility with the Executive Chairman for the agenda and the overall Board structure and composition. He will chair the Nomination Committee, provide leadership for the Independent Directors, be responsible for monitoring Board Effectiveness and lead on Corporate Governance issues. In addition, the Non-Executive Directors will meet independently at least twice a year.

d) **Appointment of two new Executive Directors and significantly enlarged responsibility for Group Finance and Operating Director** to balance responsibilities and allow Stuart to concentrate on the strategic growth areas of the business.

e) **Recruitment of an additional Non-Executive Director** to ensure a majority of independent Directors on the Board and who has the experience and credentials to become a future Senior Independent Director. Following the appointment of that Non-Executive Director, the Board will consider the appointment of a further Non-Executive Director who would also have scope to take a future senior role on the Board.

f) **Annual voting by shareholders for Stuart's re-appointment as a Director** starting in 2008, as opposed to the normal three-year cycle.

Source: Letter written by the then-Chairman of M&S to the shareholders (Lord Burns, April 2008)

Note that the full copy of the letter is available on the B291 website.

Feedback

Shareholders and institutional investors will be concerned about the concentration of power in the hands of one individual. A chairman is usually expected to be an influential non-executive monitor of the working of the board. Clearly, the company is trying hard to allay any fears (that the appointment of a CEO-cum-Chairman might not be perceived as being in the wider interests of the company) by suggesting that this would be only a short-term arrangement until 2011. To ensure that the CEO-cum-Chairman does not have unfettered powers to run the company, Marks & Spencer put in additional safeguard mechanisms. These additional measures included creating a post of Deputy Chairman, appointing an additional non-executive director and subjecting the re-appointment of the CEO-cum-Chairman as an executive director to annual voting by shareholders.

2.4 Other corporate governance models

The OECD represents 31 developed countries. In 1999, the OECD published its own principles of corporate governance, which emphasise the protection of shareholders and other stakeholders' rights, timely disclosure, transparency in reporting, and the responsibilities of the board. Despite a general OECD framework for corporate governance and the identification of underpinning principles, considerable differences prevail even among its member countries. In the UK and the USA, for example, corporate governance mechanisms emphasise the relationship between shareholders and management. However, in other countries, such as France, Germany and the Netherlands, corporate governance mechanisms take a wider stakeholder approach to governance, aiming to balance the interests of owners, managers, major creditors (such as banks) and employees. Many French and German companies have a two-tier board structure, unlike companies in the UK and the USA. The two-tier board comprises an executive board and a supervisory board. In addition, in the Franco-German model, shareholders are not the only stakeholders whose interests are considered; the interests of other stakeholders, such as employees, creditors, suppliers and banks, are also given importance in strategic decisions. In Activity 2.4 below, go through the details of corporate governance arrangements at the German company Siemens and then do the remainder of the activity.

Activity 2.4

Visit the Siemens' website, via the link on the B291 website.

Read the information about its corporate governance and identify the key elements of their corporate governance system. (Spend around five to ten minutes on the Siemens' website.)

Feedback

You may have noted the focus on responsibility for a value-based long-term performance, which indicates a concern for profits and shareholder value. Also noteworthy is the mention of the two-tier board structure in the form of Managing and Supervisory Boards. Transparency, risk management and stakeholders (shareholders and employees) are other areas where the management considers that corporate governance mechanisms are required. You could also look at the specific compliance statements by the company with respect to the German Corporate Governance Code.

As a company incorporated in Germany, Siemens AG has to comply with the German law applicable to stock corporations in Germany and the German Corporate Governance Code. However, Siemens also complies with the applicable rules and regulations of the New York Stock Exchange since it is listed there. Some of the main differences between the US corporate governance requirements and the German governance code relate to board structure, independence of directors, remuneration of directors and requirements on the composition of different committees. For example, the following is reproduced from the Siemens' website.

Differences between German and US corporate governance requirements: Siemens example

The significant differences between our governance practices and those of U.S. domestic NYSE issuers are as follows.

Two-Tier Board

The German Stock Corporation Act requires Siemens AG to have a two-tier board structure consisting of a Managing Board and a Supervisory Board. The two-tier system provides a strict separation of management and supervision. Roles and responsibilities of each of the two boards are clearly defined by law. The composition of the Supervisory Board is determined in accordance with the Codetermination Act, which requires that one-half of the required 20 Supervisory Board members must be elected by our domestic employees. In the event of a tie vote at the Supervisory Board, the Chairman of the Supervisory Board is entitled to cast a deciding vote.

Independence

In contrast to the NYSE Standards, which require the board to affirmatively determine the independence of the individual directors with reference to specific tests of independence, German law does not require the

Supervisory Board to make such affirmative findings on an individual basis. At the same time, the Bylaws for Siemens' Supervisory Board contain several provisions to help ensure the independence of the Supervisory Board's advice and supervision. Furthermore, the members of the Supervisory and Managing Boards are strictly independent from one another; a member of one board is legally prohibited from being concurrently active on the other. Supervisory Board members have independent decision-making authority and are legally prohibited from following the direction or instruction of any affiliated party. Moreover, Supervisory Board members may not enter into advisory, service or certain other contracts with Siemens, unless approved by the Supervisory Board.

Committees

In contrast to the NYSE Standards, which require the creation of several specified board committees, composed of independent directors and operating pursuant to written charters that set forth their tasks and responsibilities, the Supervisory Board of Siemens AG has combined the functions of a nominating, compensation and corporate governance committee substantially in the Chairman's Committee and has delegated the remaining functions to the Nominating Committee.

Source: Corporate Governance report (Siemens, 2009, pp. 21–22)

As the above example of a German company shows, companies listing their shares on different stock exchanges in different countries have to comply with the local stock exchange's governance requirements. Thus, a UK company listed on the New York Stock Exchange will have to comply with its rules-based governance framework and prepare the financial statements and other reports accordingly.

Summary

In this session you learned that corporate governance is a set of mechanisms to improve the accountability of management to the stakeholders in business entities. Agency problems and corporate scandals of recent decades have further strengthened the need for good corporate governance. The session also described the main elements of the UK 2008 Combined Code for corporate governance.

You have learned about different approaches to corporate governance, in particular the difference between the rules-based and the principles-based approaches. The key differences lie in the emphasis on compulsory compliance and on particular reporting formats mandated under the rules-based approach. Under the principles-based approach, compliance implies emphasis on the voluntary adoption of best practices in corporate governance. However, voluntary adoption may become obligatory when a company wishes to be listed, as the listing requirements enforced by stock exchanges will compel adoption.

SESSION **3 The relationship between ethics, governance, the law and corporate social responsibility**

Introduction

Upon completion of Session 3 you are expected to:

- understand different viewpoints; for example, stakeholders and corporate social responsibility (CSR)
- be able to explain the meaning of CSR
- be able to discuss the relationship between corporate governance, ethics and CSR and how they interact with the legal framework for corporate and professional conduct
- understand the reporting of CSR in practice.

In Session 3 you will learn about the inter-relationship of various aspects of ethics, corporate governance, CSR and legal frameworks. The first two sessions of this unit addressed issues of ethics and governance. You learned that accountants have to understand and apply professional codes in order to deal with ethical dilemmas. The previous session discussed the need for compliance with corporate governance codes. In this session you will learn about corporate social responsibility and the reporting of CSR activities. You will learn what CSR means and how it relates to governance and ethical issues.

3.1 Stakeholders and corporate social responsibility

It has been mentioned earlier in this unit, and also in Unit 1, that there are different stakeholders in business enterprise. Let us now consider why and how business enterprise should respond to different expectations from the different stakeholders in business. Consider two extreme viewpoints. First, there is the view that the purpose of a business is to increase profits for its owners. Second, there is the view that the business enterprise should be responsible for meeting the expectations of a wider set of stakeholders comprising employees, customers, investors, suppliers, the community at large and the environment. The assumption of any particular point of view may result in different approaches to how a business is managed and governed. In Session 2, for example, much of the corporate governance discussion was based on the first view, which considers the shareholders as principal stakeholders in the business. This led to the agency problem argument and the corporate governance mechanisms, which have been adopted in the UK and the USA primarily to reduce this agency problem by proposing more effective incentive and monitoring mechanisms.

With increasing pressures from consumer groups, environment protection groups and human rights groups, corporations nowadays are expected to help deal with environmental challenges, or to support charitable causes or community projects of various kinds.

For those managing businesses, these expectations create a sense of uncertainty when it comes to engaging in activities that may be called corporate social responsibility. However, there is no exact and agreed definition of CSR. It is a contested concept. What it means depends on the way one positions the role of for-profit entities in society.

The classical economist Adam Smith (1776) argued that an individual businessman, while pursuing his self-interest to increase his profits, will create wealth for society while guided by the invisible hand of competition. To compete in the market a producer has to produce and supply a product that minimises the costs of labour, raw materials and other resources and enables that producer to compete and satisfy consumer demand. Since in a competitive market all producers try to earn profits, the process leads to the efficient use of resources in society and society gets goods supplied at the lowest prices possible. Extending from the classical view, the current dominant economic logic in free market economies dictates that the main responsibility of management is to increase shareholders' wealth, as they are the principal stakeholders.

An alternative view on the objectives of the business enterprise is the stakeholder view, which argues that business should pursue multiple objectives to meet wider stakeholder considerations. Edward Freeman, in his 1984 book *Strategic Management: A Stakeholder Perspective*, proposed what has come to be known as the stakeholder theory of the firm. A stakeholder is considered to be anyone who can be, or is, influenced by the operations of a firm in society. This implies that the stakeholders in business include not only those who are contractually or primarily interested in business, such as customers, employees, owners, lenders and suppliers, but also those who may be indirectly affected, such as the environment and society at large. Stakeholder theory therefore assumes that the objectives of business enterprise need to be concerned with the interests of all stakeholders.

The above views summarise two extreme viewpoints but there are other viewpoints that lie between these two. Peter Drucker, a leading management thinker, makes the points more clearly in his following observations:

> If we want to know what business is, we have to start with its purpose. And the purpose must lie outside the business itself. In fact, it must lie in society, since a business enterprise is an organ of society. There is only one valid definition of business purpose: to create a customer. The customer is the foundation of a business and keeps it in existence. He alone gives employment. And it is to supply the customer that society entrusts wealth producing resources to the business enterprise.
>
> (Drucker, 1954, p. 37)

Drucker emphasises that the very existence of the enterprise is justified only if it can satisfy the needs of the customer. There is a difference here between Drucker's view and the dominant economic view described above. The difference is that, unless the business enterprise is capable of serving the customer, it should not be provided with capital by the investors. However, if it does serve the customers' needs, profits are necessary to serve the owners. Drucker makes this clear in the following observation but again locates the argument for profits in a wider stakeholder perspective:

> A business that does not show a profit at least equal to its cost of capital is socially irresponsible; it wastes society's resources. Economic profit performance is the base without which business cannot discharge any other responsibilities, cannot be a good employer, a good citizen, a good neighbor. But economic performance is not the only responsibility of a business. ... Every organization must assume responsibility for its impact on employees, the environment, customers, and whomever and whatever it touches. That is social responsibility. But we know that society will increasingly look to major organizations, for-profit and non-profit alike, to tackle major social ills. And that is where we had better be watchful, because good intentions are not always socially responsible. It is irresponsible for an organization to accept—let alone pursue—responsibilities that would impede its capacity to perform its main task and mission or to act where it has no competence.
>
> (Drucker, 2002a)

The above statement by Drucker shows how the profit motive links to the achievement of various societal objectives. First is the waste of capital resources. Refer to the earlier observations where Drucker argues that society entrusts its resources to business enterprise to make use of them to produce goods for customers. However, if the business enterprise does not earn sufficient profits to meet the cost of the capital provided, it is a waste of society's resources. Other social responsibilities of business can be satisfied only if the economic performance is good. Drucker also states that business enterprise should not pursue social objectives that it may not be able to deliver. Drucker defined more clearly in his other book, *A Functioning Society*, how the multidimensional performance implied in stakeholder theory could be measured:

> We no longer need to theorize about how to define performance and results in the large enterprise. We have successful examples ... They do not 'balance' anything. They maximize. But they do not attempt to maximize shareholder value or the short-term interest of any one of the enterprise's 'stakeholders.' Rather, they maximize the wealth-producing capacity of the enterprise. It is this objective that integrates the short-term and long-term results and that ties the operational dimensions of business performance—market standing, innovation, productivity, and people and their development—with the financial needs and financial results. It is also this objective on which all the constituencies—whether shareholders, customers, or employees—depend for the satisfaction of their expectations and objectives.
>
> (Drucker, 2002b)

The above description provides a broad background perspective from the economic and stakeholder theory perspectives that underpin much of the debate on CSR. In Section 3.2 we consider in greater detail the meaning of CSR, using one of the many models that have been proposed for understanding CSR.

3.2 Understanding corporate social responsibility

One definition that closely follows from Drucker's exposition of the concept of social responsibility and is in line with economic and stakeholder theories is given by Archie Carroll: 'corporate social responsibility of business entails the simultaneous fulfilment of the firm's economic, legal, ethical, and philanthropic responsibilities. Stated in more pragmatic and managerial terms, the CSR firm should strive to *make a profit, obey the law, be ethical,* and *be a good corporate citizen*' (Carroll, 1991). This is a comprehensive definition of CSR showing that the scope of CSR activities is more than just following all relevant laws of the land, ensuring ethical conduct of business and compliance with best practices in the corporate governance framework applicable in the given country. A distinguishing feature of CSR relates to the voluntary nature of the CSR activities. In other words, CSR represents contributions by business entities to community projects and activities, not because of legal, ethical or governance requirements but because of organisational commitment to wider societal and environmental interests. The voluntary nature of CSR is recognised by academic scholars and policy makers. For example, the European Commission defines CSR as, '*a concept whereby companies integrate social and environmental concerns in their business operations and in their interaction with their stakeholders on a voluntary basis.*'

In summary, we can say that CSR is a voluntary set of activities that a corporation engages in to support social, economic, and environmental causes that are not legal, fiduciary, ethical or corporate governance requirements.

3.3 CSR, ethics, governance and law

As the foregoing discussion shows, the scope of CSR activities overlaps with society's expectations of companies to conduct their business ethically and in accordance with best corporate governance practices. One way to understand the relationship between CSR, ethics, governance and law could be to think of the issues as lying on a continuum of obligation from a legal requirement to management discretion. For example, legal requirements to invest in pollution control systems are obligatory whereas a company's policy to procure raw materials from sustainable resources may be considered socially responsible behaviour.

Table 1 depicts a conceptual framework that is one way to show the links between CSR, ethics and law. The table shows that while economic efficiency and profitability are necessary, the four sets of expectations from corporations are not necessarily sequential or hierarchical. A business enterprise is expected to make profits but without disobeying the law on minimum wages, for example. However, as discussed above, although the management of a corporation has obligations to obey the law, there is likely to be an element of choice involved in the extent and type of CSR activities that a corporation supports.

Table 1 Responsibilities of business

ECONOMIC responsibilities	Be profitable.
	The foundation on which the business enterprise makes sure it can continue to exist and that it can meet ethical and philanthropic responsibilities.
LEGAL responsibilities	Obey the law.
	Law is society's codification of right and wrong. Play by the rules of the game.
ETHICAL responsibilities	Be ethical.
	Obligation to do what is right, just, and fair. Avoid harm.
PHILANTHROPIC responsibilities	Be a good corporate citizen.
	Contribute resources to the community; improve quality of life.

Source: Adapted from 'The pyramid of corporate social responsibility: toward the moral management of organizational stakeholders' (Carroll, 1991).

3.4 Reporting CSR in practice

In the business environment, with all its economic uncertainties, competition and the challenges of managing large corporations, managers' jobs are complex. In addition to these challenges, expecting corporations to take a view on CSR obligations can mean that managing sometimes competing stakeholder claims on business just increases the complexity of decision making. The pressures on business managers from various stakeholders, including government and non-government organisations, have increased. Responding to various stakeholder expectations, many companies now report on their CSR activities. Therefore, it is worth understanding the various types of reports in this context. Consider the following three definitions of inter-related reports that many companies now publish as separate documents or as part of their annual report. These definitions of social responsibility reports, green reports and social audit reports provide an over-arching understanding of what constitutes CSR reporting.

3.4.1 Social responsibility report

This is generally part of the annual report, as you will see in the illustration of Marks & Spencer later in this session. According to one definition, such a report includes: 'the costs to the business of e.g. equipment donated, sponsorship given, or charitable donations. The monetary quantification of social benefits is much harder to measure and necessarily subjective. Owing to the concerns of consumers, investors, and other stakeholders, companies are increasingly obliged to be environmentally and socially conscious' (Law and Owen, 1999). As can be seen in this explanation, the issues covered include environmental and social issues.

3.4.2   Green report

This is defined as a 'report by the directors of a company that attempts to quantify the costs and benefits of that company's operations in relation to the environment' (Law and Owen, 1999). In the UK there is a move towards the development of carbon trust standards, which will be based on an independent assessment of an enterprise's 'carbon footprint' – a term generally meaning the impact of organisational activities on the environment. At present the idea is promoted as good practice, but if carbon standards are made into legal requirements in the UK this will have an impact on UK-based companies as they will have to invest in technologies and processes to meet the environmental standards. This, in turn, would require reporting that explicitly recognises the environmental costs and benefits of businesses.

Both corporate social responsibility and green reports require that organisations should put in place processes to prepare such reports. Social audit and environmental audit are two such processes.

3.4.3   Social and environmental audits

Social audit is an audit of the impact of an organisation on society, which covers different stakeholders. Environmental audit is an audit of the impact of an organisation's activities on the environment. Its purpose is usually to ensure that the organisation has clear environmental policies, that its operations comply with the stated environmental policies, and that its policies are subject to regular review. Environmental audits may be conducted internally or externally by environmental consultants (Law and Owen, 1999). The UK Auditing Practices Board (2009b) defines the related environmental performance report as '[a] report, separate from the financial statements, in which an entity provides third parties with qualitative information on the entity's commitments towards the environmental aspects of the business, its policies and targets in that field, its achievement in managing the relationship between its business processes and environmental risk, and quantitative information on its environmental performance'.

Many companies now report on their CSR activities in their annual reports. In some cases CSR activities are part of a company's strategic choices, as seems apparent from the following five year plan drawn up by Marks & Spencer as part of their commitment to social and environmental initiatives.

Marks & Spencer CSR initiatives

We launched Plan A in January 2007, setting out 100 commitments to achieve in 5 years. ... Through Plan A we are working with our customers and our suppliers to combat climate change, reduce waste, use sustainable raw materials, trade ethically, and help our customers to lead healthier lifestyles.

For more information about the M&S five year plan, visit http://plana.marksandspencer.com/about (accessed 14 October 2010).

Activity 3.1

Do the various activities under M&S Plan A cover only corporate social responsibility issues or do they overlap with ethics, law and governance issues? Explain your answer.

You do not need to read all of the M&S Plan A to do this activity; the extract provided is sufficient. The website link is mentioned only if you are interested in knowing more. (Spend no more than five minutes on this activity.)

Feedback

You have probably noted that the scope of activities listed in Plan A go beyond legal, ethics and governance codes. This shows the difficulty of defining corporate social responsibility, as it seems to encompass a wide range of activities that could be classified as CSR.

Marks & Spencer is not the only company that seems to be proactive in its response to social and environmental responsibilities. Many other companies around the world have responded to changing expectations from consumer groups, government agencies and environmental groups and have engaged in ethical, social and environmentally acceptable business practices. Actually, in the reporting environment, CSR is almost an expected report rather than a matter of choice for most companies. This is because many pressure groups monitor and highlight the information and events that concern the socially responsible behaviour of companies. The following article demonstrates that companies have shown sustained commitment to such activities even in the difficult market conditions that followed the 2007–08 global economic recession.

Why corporate responsibility is a survivor

It was an easy prediction to make: that the recession would end talk of corporate social responsibility. Faced with the fear, or reality, of losing their jobs or homes, consumers would rush past the Fairtrade shelves and pick up something the family could afford. Companies, meanwhile, would concentrate on saving themselves rather than the planet.

That easy prediction has turned out to be wrong. Mars, the world's biggest confectionery company, has announced that its entire cocoa supply will be 'produced in a sustainable manner' by 2020. Mars will work largely with the Rainforest Alliance, which encourages farmers to preserve their environment.

Mars's move follows the announcement last month by Cadbury, the UK confectionery group, that all the cocoa in Dairy Milk, Britain's biggest-selling chocolate, would be certified by Fairtrade, the organisation that works to ensure a minimum price for farmers.[1]

The two chocolate makers were preceded by Wal-Mart, the world's biggest retailer, which told a meeting of 1,000 Chinese suppliers last year that it would hold them to strict environmental and social standards, the downturn notwithstanding.

Why are these companies acting in a way few expected? First, there are substantial business reasons. When Mars and Cadbury talk about their cocoa supplies being sustainable, they mean it. Chocolate manufacturers are worried about how much cocoa will be available a decade from now. Worldwide cocoa production fell in 2008 for the fourth successive year. Cadbury says it is worried about how few cocoa farmers' children intend to go into the business. It is hoping the investment in farms that Fairtrade encourages will persuade them cocoa farming is a worthwhile occupation.

Wal-Mart also has commercial reasons for its stance. The company has been encouraging companies to cut down on packaging. This enables it to fit more goods into each delivery truck, not only reducing its emissions, but also cutting the amount it spends on petrol. Its insistence that manufacturers produce concentrated laundry detergent has allowed it to save on both packaging and shelf space. Cost-cutting is vital to beating the downturn and if companies can boost their green credentials at the same time, why not?

But the companies go further. Not only do their announcements make business sense, they say; consumers, even now, insist on them. Fiona Dawson, Mars UK's managing director, says customers expect the company to 'do the right thing', adding that 'nobody has to buy confectionery'.

There are many things that consumers do not have to buy, and plenty they can buy more cheaply. As the Financial Times has reported, US families earning more than $100,000 a year are using more discount coupons.

Yet there is little sign of committed consumers abandoning Fairtrade products. A recent report by Mintel, the research organisation, says: 'Although a third of shoppers have cut down on the number of premium foods they buy, only one in 10 has cut back on ethical produce.' Justin King, chief executive of J Sainsbury, the UK retailer, said in February that its Fairtrade sales were holding up well.

However, consumer attitudes are complex. Mike Barry, head of corporate social responsibility at rival retailer Marks and Spencer, says consumers are happy to continue to buy what they see as ethically sourced goods – provided they do not have to pay more. M&S's research says the number of 'green crusaders' – those who buy

ethical goods, no matter what, is about 9 per cent of the total, slightly down from the proportion at the start of the recession.

About a fifth of consumers are uninterested in such issues and about a third cannot see what difference their purchasing makes. But the biggest group, about 40 per cent, are those who are prepared to buy ethical goods if companies make it easy, which generally means not making it expensive.

As Fairtrade involves paying producers more, how can retailers keep the prices competitive? Mr Barry says that when, in 2007, M&S laid out its 'Plan A' on sustainable sourcing and fair trading, it expected the changes to cost the company £200m ($290m, €225m) over five years. But because, like Wal-Mart, M&S is saving money through its initiatives, it is finding its changes are cost-neutral.

This is the key to companies' stubborn adherence to corporate social responsibility. They have worked out how to make it pay. Many of their initiatives help to cut costs or sustain supplies. They allow customers to continue to regard themselves as ethical during difficult times. They also help the companies to improve their public reputations at a time when business is widely held to be responsible for the downturn.

A pre-recession argument for corporate responsibility was that it gave companies a moral 'licence to operate'. Some sceptics regarded this as a bit of a joke. Few do now.

Source: *Financial Times* (Skapinker, M., 2009)

[1] Cadbury was taken over by Kraft Inc. of the USA in 2010.

Activity 3.2 ....

After reading the above article, do you think that companies are driven by only commercial reasons to undertake and support CSR initiatives or are there other reasons as well? (Spend no more than ten minutes on this activity.)

Feedback ....

The article provides clear examples of commercial reasons, such as the sustainable supply of raw materials like cocoa. However, there are consumer pressures too that seem to push companies towards CSR activities. The reputational advantages are another incentive for companies to engage in corporate social responsibility.

Summary

In this session you learned about the meaning of corporate social responsibility. The academic definition of CSR and reporting of CSR activities by companies shows that CSR tends to overlap with the ethical, governance and legal aspects of business. CSR is also closely tied in with the stakeholder debate whereby businesses are expected to balance the interests of various stakeholders in business. Finally, the reporting of CSR takes different forms, such as the social responsibility report and the environmental report.

In the next session you will learn about internal controls. It goes into greater detail about management accountability for managing risk, as indicated in Session 2 on corporate governance (by reference there to the UK Combined Code and other governance codes).

SESSION 4 Internal and external audit

Introduction

In Session 2 you learned about the need for and scope of corporate governance. An internal control system is integral to effective corporate governance. In this session you will learn more about internal control, and the meaning of internal audit and external audit in the context of internal control. This session also helps you to understand the prevention of accounting-related fraud in the context of internal control.

Upon completion of Session 4 you are expected to be able to:

- discuss the need for and scope of internal controls
- explain the scope and elements of internal and external audit
- discuss the differences between external and internal audit.

The internal and external environments in which business entities operate keep changing. Internal environment includes the organisation structure, policies, procedures and technologies, etc., that the company uses. External environment includes the regulatory and legal environment and competition. Change offers new opportunities and new challenges. A business entity, therefore, needs to be in a position to identify and manage any internal and external risks that may arise. Most business operations do involve a certain degree of risk. For example, the actual demand for a product in a particular year may turn out to be less than expected at the start of the year. This may result in lower profits, which in turn may affect the company's share price. A sound internal control system may not eliminate such risks but it can help to reduce or manage them better. That is why it is argued that internal control has an important role in the management of risks that are significant to the fulfilment of organisational objectives.

4.1 The meaning of and need for internal control

As part of good governance practice the management of an entity is expected to develop risk assessment processes, together with information and reporting systems that help management to control and monitor organisational performance. Effective control systems require detailed planning and execution. The Turnbull Report, published in the UK in 1999 (revised in 2005), provided guidance for directors regarding internal controls. The Turnbull Report (full title: *Internal Control Revised Guidance for Directors on the Combined Code*) forms the basis of the recommendations on internal control set out in the UK Combined Code.

The UK Combined Code recommends that the management of an entity should provide a sound control system to safeguard shareholders' investments and assets. The Code also recommends that the board should conduct a review of the effectiveness of a company's system of internal controls at least annually and should report to shareholders that they have done so. The review should cover all material controls, including financial, operational and compliance controls, and risk management systems. All this is done by creating an appropriate control environment and putting in place effective financial controls and internal audit and risk management processes and procedures. The purposes of internal control for an entity are described below. They:

- *facilitate its effective and efficient operation* by enabling the entity to respond appropriately to significant business, operational, financial, compliance and other risks to achieving the company's objectives. This includes safeguarding assets from inappropriate use or from loss and fraud and ensuring that liabilities are identified and managed

- *help ensure the quality of internal and external reporting*. This requires the maintenance of proper records and processes that generate a flow of timely, relevant and reliable information from within and outside the organisation

- *help ensure compliance* with applicable laws and regulations, and also with internal policies with respect to the conduct of business.

To achieve the above objectives many entities set up an audit committee or an Internal Controls Committee with a clear mandate to examine the working of the internal control systems and to work with the board of directors to make the internal control systems effective.

The international standard on auditing (ISA 315) deals with the responsibility of auditors to identify and assess material misstatements in financial statements. For this purpose the auditors are required to understand the entity and its environment, including the entity's internal control. Internal control is 'the process designed, implemented and maintained by those charged with governance, management and other personnel to provide reasonable assurance about the achievement of an entity's objectives with regard to reliability of financial reporting, effectiveness and efficiency of operations, and compliance with applicable laws and regulations' (ISA 315 (Redrafted), p. 55).

Who sets auditing standards?

International Standards of Auditing (ISAs) are prepared by The International Auditing and Assurance Standards Board (IAASB), which is part of The International Federation of Accountants (IFAC). The ISAs promulgated by IAASB are typically adopted at national level by the national audit standard setters wherever they exist. (You can visit the IAASB website via the link on the B291 website.)

In the UK the Auditing Practices Board establishes the auditing standards, which are called International Standards on Auditing, UK and Ireland (ISA (UK and Ireland)). The Auditing Practices Board is part of the Financial Reporting Council in the UK.

Activity 4.1

Read the following extract from the 2009 annual report of a UK-based company. De La Rue, the world's largest commercial security printer and papermaker, is involved in the production of over 150 national currencies and a wide range of security documents, such as passports, authentication labels and fiscal stamps. Around the world, central banks use De La Rue equipment to count and sort notes quickly, reliably and in large quantities, helping them to reduce the cost of handling cash. De La Rue also pioneers new technologies in government identity solutions for national identification, driver's licence and passport issuing schemes.

De La Rue Annual Report 2009

Business Review: Risk and Risk Management

De La Rue's reputation is based on security, integrity and trust. This section therefore only summarises the types of risks which are either specific to the continuing businesses of De La Rue or which could have a material, adverse effect on the Group, following the disposal of the Cash Systems business. It also describes the risk management systems and processes in place and significant events during 2008/2009.

No business is risk free even if it has detailed processes and procedures for identifying and managing risks. The Combined Code on Corporate Governance requires the Board to maintain a sound system of internal control to safeguard shareholders' investment and the Company's assets and at least annually to conduct a review of the effectiveness of the Group's system of internal controls. The Board carried out its annual review which covered all material controls, including financial, operational and compliance controls and risk management systems. Additionally, the Board received information about the Group's operations throughout the year enabling it regularly to evaluate the nature and extent of the risks to which the Company is exposed. The Board is therefore able to confirm that its system of internal control has been in place throughout 2008/2009.

Internal Control and Internal Financial Control

The Board has overall responsibility for the Group's system of internal control and for reviewing its effectiveness. It relies on the Audit Committee and Risk Committee to assist in this process. Details of the Audit and Risk Committees are set out in the Corporate Governance Statement.

Source: De La Rue Annual Report 2009 (p. 34).

Note down your answers to each of the following questions:

1   Who will be providing key information and analysis to the board of De La Rue regarding the risks to which the company may be exposed?

2   Considering the nature of the business in which De La Rue operates, what could be a major risk that a company like De La Rue could face internally?

3   Considering the nature of the business in which De La Rue operates, what could be a major risk that a company like De La Rue could face externally?

(Spend about ten minutes on this activity.)

Feedback ....

4.2 Elements of internal control

The control environment in corporations includes the governance structure and management functions as well as the attitudes, awareness and actions of those charged with the governance and management of the entity's internal control and its importance in the entity. The Turnbull Report (2005) on internal controls goes into great detail about the best practices on internal control for UK listed companies and provides guidance on how these should be applied. The key elements of internal control are as follows (adapted from Appendix 2 of ISA 315 (pp. 48–50)):

The UK Combined Code and the Turnbull Report on guidance for internal control systems can be accessed via the www.frc.org.uk link on the B291 website, as can texts of ISAs (UK and Ireland) through the link to the Auditing Practices Board.

1   *Communication and enforcement of integrity and ethical values.* An effective control environment requires that ethical behaviour and integrity are enforced throughout the organisation. For this to happen, the management of the entity needs to communicate the ethical standards to all the members of the organisation and create the structure, develop the procedures, systems and incentives that support ethical conduct within the organisation. These include management's actions to remove incentives and temptations that might prompt personnel to engage in dishonest, illegal or unethical acts.

2   *Commitment to competence.* Commitment to competence includes management's consideration of the competence levels for particular jobs and how those levels translate into requisite skills and knowledge.

3   *Participation by those charged with governance.* In Session 2 of this unit you learned that independent (non-executive) directors are expected to take responsibility for scrutinising and monitoring the internal control and internal audit processes. These responsibilities include oversight of the design and effective operation of whistle-blower procedures (whereby any employee could report anything that they think violates the company's policies on good governance) and the process for reviewing the effectiveness of the entity's internal control systems.

4   *Management's philosophy and operating style.* Management's philosophy and operating style encompass management's approach to taking and monitoring business risks, management's attitudes and actions towards financial reporting, and management's attitudes toward information processing, accounting functions and personnel.

5   *Organisational structure*. Organisational structure provides a framework for implementing organisational strategies, procedures and policies to achieve organisational objectives. A suitable organisational structure is important to ensure that internal controls are implemented.

6   *Assignment of authority and responsibility*. Implicit in organisational structure design is the assignment of authority and responsibility for operating activities. Assignment of authority and responsibility includes the definitions of roles and responsibilities of individuals and their reporting relationships.

7   *Human resource policies and practices*. As already mentioned, people play an important role in creating an effective control environment. Hence recruitment, training and performance appraisal policies must ensure that an organisation attracts, trains and retains people who are competent and meet the organisational standards of integrity and ethics.

A sound internal control system should be embedded in the operations of the company and should be part of its organisational culture. This is necessary to ensure that the system is equipped to identify and respond to risks arising from the internal and external business environment. This, therefore, makes it necessary that the system include the following.

* identification and allocation of responsibilities for control activities

* information and communications processes

* processes for monitoring the continuing effectiveness of the system of internal controls.

Activity 4.2

Read through the internal and financial control procedures and responsibilities in the case of De La Rue as reported by the company in its annual report for 2009. Then respond to the following requirements:

1   Consider the information provided by De La Rue about its internal control system and briefly comment on how it relates to the elements for control environment described earlier.

2   What are the three main types of control procedure described in the extract from the De La Rue report?

(Spend about ten to fifteen minutes on this activity.)

De La Rue internal control systems

Management is responsible for implementing the controls which are designed to meet the particular needs of the Group, and the risks to which it is exposed, with procedures intended to provide effective internal control. Business Unit Managing Directors, to whom general managers of smaller businesses report, are responsible for establishing and maintaining these procedures.

The controls by their nature are designed to manage rather than eliminate risk and can only provide reasonable but not absolute assurance against material misstatement or loss. The processes used by the Board and, on its behalf, by the Audit and Risk Committees have been in place throughout the year, and include:

* reviewing:
  * monthly finance, operational and development reports
  * internal and external audit plans

○   significant issues identified by internal and external audits

○   significant Group risks and risk mitigation actions reported by the Risk Committee including updates to the Group's risk register

○   annual compliance statements in the form of self-audit questionnaires

○   reports on other such matters as security, health and safety, environmental issues and fire risks.

• discussing with management risks identified by management and/or the audit process and any changes from the previous review.

The financial control framework includes the following key features:

• an annual strategic planning process
• an annual budget
• a system of monthly reporting by each operating subsidiary which involves comparison of actual results with the original budget and the updating of a full year forecast
• monthly reporting of performance to the Board
• audited annual financial statements
• interim financial statements reviewed by the auditors.

The main control procedures which address the financial implications of the major business risks are centred on strict approval procedures. These are reviewed annually, approved by the Board and apply to all subsidiaries. They include:

• executive Directors' approval of all major non-routine revenue expenditure
• Board approval of all major capital expenditure
• Board approval of all acquisitions and disposals
• a system of authorisation limits which cascades throughout the Group
• Board consideration of any matter having a material effect on the Group.

Following the disposal of Cash Systems, the internal audit function was outsourced entirely to Ernst & Young who have, in conjunction with senior management and the Audit Committee, carried out a review of the focus of, and way in which, internal audits will be carried out in the future with the objective of targeting resources better and improving the process.

Source: De La Rue Annual Report 2009 (pp. 34–5).

Feedback ....

1   You may have noted that nearly all the elements of control environment are found in De La Rue's description of its internal controls. The first paragraph identifies who is responsible for implementing the controls (points 3 and 6 in the text). The authority and responsibility for designing and implementing the internal controls spans from the Board down to general managers of smaller businesses. The processes and procedures include an on-going review process. The final paragraph hints at the company's recognition that they need to improve the processes further.

2   The three types of control are:

(i) non-financial review and monitoring reports such as group risk reports, compliance reports and other such reports

(ii) financial control reports such as budgets, financial plans and financial performance reports

(iii) approval and authorisation of major decisions by the senior management.

One of the key elements of internal control is a continuous review of the effectiveness of internal control systems. Internal audit, therefore, is considered to be an important part of internal control. In the following section you will learn about the relationship between the audit and internal control systems and also the functions of audit.

4.3 External audit

In this section you will learn about why auditors are needed and how they relate to internal control systems. You will learn about the meaning of audit and its aims. It is worth noting that internal auditors may be either the employees of a company or audit consultants hired for this purpose. Then there are external auditors who are independent auditors hired by a company to audit financial statements. As explained below there are significant differences between the roles of external audit and internal audit in corporate governance.

4.3.1 Meaning, purpose and scope of external audit

There is a similar organisation in the UK called The British Accounting Association (BAA).

A committee constituted by the American Accounting Association (AAA, a voluntary organisation for the promotion of accounting education, research and practice) and called the Committee on Basic Auditing Concepts (1969–71) defined auditing as 'a systematic process of objectively obtaining and evaluating evidence regarding assertions about economic actions and events to ascertain the degree of correspondence between those assertions and established criteria and communicating the results to interested users.' This definition implies a wide scope for an auditor's responsibilities. In the UK, the *Companies Act 2006* and the International Auditing Standards list several responsibilities of external auditors. These are described below.

> An audit involves obtaining evidence about the amounts and disclosures in the financial statements sufficient to give reasonable assurance that the financial statements are free from material misstatement, whether caused by fraud or error. This includes an assessment of: whether the accounting policies are appropriate to the [group and the parent] company's circumstances and have been consistently applied and adequately disclosed; the reasonableness of significant accounting estimates made by the directors; and the overall presentation of the financial statements.
>
> (Auditing Practices Board, 2009a)

The *Companies Act 2006* (in *s.495*) requires the auditor to make a formal report (called an audit report) to the company's members that must state clearly whether, in the auditor's opinion, the financial statements:

- give a true and fair view in the case of an individual balance sheet, of the state of affairs of the company as at the end of the financial year
- give a true and fair view in the case of an individual income statement, of the profit or loss of the company for the financial year

- give a true and fair view in the case of group accounts, of the state of affairs as at the end of the financial year and of the profit or loss for the financial year of the undertakings included in the consolidation as a whole, so far as concerns members of the company
- have been properly prepared in accordance with the relevant financial reporting framework
- have been prepared in accordance with the requirements of *Companies Act 2006* and, in the case of the consolidated accounts of publicly traded companies, the requirements of Article 4 of the IAS Regulation.

The *Companies Act 2006* further requires the auditor's report on the financial statements to be either unqualified or qualified and to include a reference to any matters to which the auditor wishes to draw attention by way of emphasis without qualifying the report.

Activity 4.3 ....

The assurance provided by an external audit may be of value not only to the shareholders but also to other stakeholders. Can you remember any other groups that have been mentioned previously that may use audited financial statements? (Spend no more than ten minutes on this activity.)

Feedback ....

Your list might have included:

- potential shareholders or investors
- lenders of capital
- employees or trade unions for wage negotiations
- financial analysts and advisers
- customers and suppliers for credit rating purposes
- business advisers such as consultants
- government agencies for tax purposes and other government departments for macroeconomic planning and national statistics.

4.3.2   What constitutes a true and fair view?

You should now begin to sense what is meant by a 'true and fair view'. Maybe not? Unfortunately, although the *Companies Act 2006* requires the financial statements to show a true and fair view, *it does not define what a true and fair view is*! In the UK, the Financial Reporting Council (FRC) has sought legal opinions to clarify the meaning of the 'true and fair' concept. In 1983 and 1984 opinions were sought from Lord Hoffmann and Dame Mary Arden. In 2008 the FRC further sought the views of Martin Moore QC subsequent to the implementation of the *Companies Act 2006*. Martin Moore endorsed the opinions expressed by Lord Hoffmann and Dame Mary Arden and summarised his opinion as follows:

These opinions are available from the Financial Reporting Council website.

> The true and fair view, or fair presentation, concept is of an overarching nature. Any decision made or judgement reached by the preparer of financial statements is not made in a vacuum but is made against the requirement to give a true and fair view, or to achieve a fair presentation.

(Moore, 2008)

Elaborating this further Martin Moore QC illustrates below how the dynamic nature of the 'true and fair' concept 'comes into play':

- in the way in which a standard is applied,
- in consideration of whether a standard should be departed from in those 'exceptional' or 'extremely rare' cases in which departure is permitted,
- in the choices regarding the applicability of a particular standard, or
- in determining the closest analogy where the circumstances are not precisely covered by a standard.

(Moore, 2008)

In the auditing context the two key words *true* and *fair* can be interpreted as follows.

1   *True* implies that financial information is factual and conforms to reality; that it complies with law and accounting standards and that the accounts have been correctly extracted from the company's books and records.

2   *Fair* implies that the financial information is not subject to discrimination and bias, and is in compliance with accounting standards; the accounts should reflect the commercial substance of the company's underlying transactions.

The foregoing description of the 'true and fair' concepts shows that accounting truth is not the same as scientific truth. Financial statements are always based on subjective judgement. It is unlikely that two accountants working independently on the same financial information would produce an identical set of financial statements. They will, for example, have different views on materiality: one will check differences of any amount between individual items and other evidence, whereas another will ignore such differences if they are below a specified amount. Also, the periodic depreciation charge on an asset will differ depending on whether the straight-line or reducing balance method is used, and depending on what residual value was set for the asset in question.

Activity 4.4   ....

In order for financial statements to show a true and fair view, do they have to be completely correct, right down to the last penny?

Perhaps this example will help you. You are auditing a company's accounts and are now looking at the Cash Book. You discover that the balance of money in the bank is three pence more in the Cash Book than it is in the bank statement. You have checked every entry in the Cash Book with the entries in the bank statement. Still, the difference remains.

Think carefully about this. It is a far more contentious and important point than you might expect. (Spend about ten minutes on this activity.)

Feedback   ....

Of course, there must have been an error in the entries in either the Cash Book or the bank statement. You would find it if you spent long enough looking for it. Auditors need to decide whether it is worth spending many hours looking for differences like these. Most of them would not because financial statements do not have to be 100 per cent correct to reflect a true and fair view.

Recall that a true and fair view means that the accounts have complied with the relevant country's statutes and International Financial Reporting Standards where applicable. Errors, omissions and misstatements may be present but these should not be material. This means that such things within the accounts will not mislead the users of the accounts or materially misrepresent the financial position of the company. This said, an error that appears non-material might actually conceal a material error. You learned about various types of accounting errors in Unit 4. One of the types of error you learned about was called a compensating error. Consider that such an error of £1,000,000 was compensated by another error of £1,000,000.03 giving a net difference of only 3 pence. On its face value 3 pence appears non-material but the actual error involves much larger sums that will need correction.

4.3.3   The scope of external audit

Large entities other than traditional companies also require an annual external audit. These entities include those in Table 2 below.

Table 2   External audit for different types of entity

Entity	Relevant legislation
Limited Companies	*Companies Act 2006*
Building Societies	*Building Societies Act 1986*
Trade Unions and Employers Associations	*Trade Union and Labour Relations (Consolidation) Act 1992*
Housing Associations	Various, according to the legal constitution of the housing association
Charities (some)	Various, dependent on the nature and legal form of the charity
Unincorporated investment business	*Financial Services and Markets Act 2000*

Solicitors and pension funds also have their own legislation, and public sector organisations have their own framework for external audit. According to *s.477* of the *Companies Act 2006,* small companies are exempt from having their financial statements audited by an external auditor. To qualify as a small company, *SI 2008/393 The Companies Act 2006 (Amendment) (Accounts and Reports) Regulations 2008* defines a small company as one that satisfies two of the following conditions. The discussion here is kept simple and at an introductory level.

1   turnover during the year is not more than £6.5 million
2   balance sheet does not total more than £3.26 million
3   number of employees is not more than 50.

(The UK *Companies Act 2006* provides further details about thresholds on the amounts for turnover and aggregate totals. There are provisions about the first year of the company and subsequent years, and also provisions with respect to a parent company, etc.)

Entities that do not have to go through an annual external audit – for example, partnerships, sole traders and clubs – may still wish an independent auditor to examine their accounts. When this is done, it is known as a non-statutory audit.

Activity 4.5   ....

Non-statutory audits obviously cost money. What reasons can you think of that would persuade a partnership to undergo a non-statutory audit? Write a list of possible reasons in the space below. (Spend no more than ten minutes on this activity.)

Feedback   ....

- Profit sharing between partners is settled equitably, especially if complicated profit-sharing arrangements exist.
- Audited partnership financial statements facilitate the admission of new partner(s) if a set of credible previous accounts exist.
- Partnership changes initiated by a change in the profit-sharing ratios, death or retirement of partners are facilitated. These may result in asset revaluations and the recognition and distribution of goodwill between partners. Figures will be given credibility if the financial statements are audited after they have been adjusted.
- Applications to third parties for loan finance are enhanced if supported by audited financial statements.
- Audited financial statements submitted to the tax authorities carry greater credibility.

4.3.4   External audit and corporate governance

The need to appoint an external auditor is enforced by the *Companies Act 2006* in the UK and by similar legislation in other countries. The UK *Companies Act* requires that:

- directors must account for the stewardship of the assets under their control to the shareholders
- the financial statements must be examined by independent auditors who must report to the shareholders whether the financial statements present a true and fair view of the financial position of the business.

The first requirement refers to a similar expectation that is also expressed in the Combined Code. The second requirement is a legal corporate governance mechanism that existed for a long time before the Combined Code was developed. Every limited company is required by law to prepare annual accounts that report on the financial performance and activities of the company during the year. As you know, this period is generally referred to as a financial year. All limited companies must send (or 'file') a copy of a set of their financial statements to the Registrar of Companies. Some companies need to file only abbreviated financial statements.

In the UK, per *s.442(2) Companies Act 2006*, in the case of private limited companies the financial statements must be nine months after the end of the company's accounting period whereas public limited companies have only six months within which to comply. To satisfy these requirements all companies are required to keep accounting records to enable the final accounts to be prepared. The responsibility for the preparation of these accounts lies with the company's directors. The accounting records in particular must:

- show with reasonable accuracy, at any time during the financial year, the financial position of the company at that time
- enable the directors to ensure that any balance sheet and income statement prepared by them gives a true and fair view of the company's profit or loss.

The directors of public limited companies are normally not the owners of the company. This phenomenon is known as the 'separation of ownership and management control', discussed earlier in the unit in regard to the agency relationship. The directors are appointed by the owners (i.e., the shareholders) to manage the company on their behalf. The directors do so by fulfilling a duty of stewardship. Since the owners do not participate actively in the operational management of the companies, they want to know that the financial statements present a true and fair view. In order to do so, an independent external auditor is appointed by the shareholders to examine and confirm whether the financial statements present a true and fair view; that is, whether the financial statements, as prepared by the directors, fairly reflect the performance and financial position of the company.

4.4 The purpose and scope of internal audit

As part of their internal financial control mechanisms, it is desirable that companies introduce a specific management control function known as internal audit. The Institute of Internal Auditors (2010) defines internal audit as:

> An independent, objective assurance and consulting activity designed to add value and improve an organisation's operations. It helps an organisation accomplish its objectives by bringing a systematic, disciplined approach to evaluate and improve the effectiveness of risk management, control, and governance processes.

The Auditing Practices Board (2009b) in the UK defines internal audit as:

> An appraisal activity established within an entity as a service to the entity. Its functions include, amongst other things, examining, evaluating and monitoring the adequacy and effectiveness of internal control.

It is a statutory requirement that publicly traded companies maintain an internal audit function. More recently, the increasing demands of corporate governance have raised the profile of internal audit. The Turnbull Report (2005) in the UK suggested that the need for an internal function would vary depending on company-specific factors. These factors include:

- the scale, diversity and complexity of the company's activities
- the number of employees
- the cost-benefit of introducing an internal audit
- changes in the company's internal and external operating environment that may have increased the risks or changed the nature of activities, which require changes in the internal control systems including internal audit.

If an internal audit function does exist, the external auditor may liaise with those involved in order to maximise audit coverage.

4.4.1 What does an internal auditor do?

The internal audit function has been evolving with the increasing size and complexity of business that many large companies have experienced over decades. The recommendations in the UK Combined Code have had a major impact on the role of the internal auditor, resulting in both a widening of the role of internal audit to encompass managing the whole of the business risks, and an increase in the status of the internal auditor. After the emergence of governance codes in many countries, most large companies include an internal audit function as part of the internal control framework to help ensure compliance with the governance code and to strengthen internal control mechanisms. The UK Combined Code recommends that the board should establish an audit committee of at least three independent directors or, in the case of smaller companies, two independent directors. According to Sir Robert Smith's 2003 report on Audit Committees, the purpose of such a committee should be as set out below, namely:

- to monitor the integrity of the financial statements of the company
- to review the company's internal financial control system and, unless addressed by a separate risk committee or by the board itself, risk management systems
- to monitor and review the effectiveness of the company's internal audit function
- to make recommendations to the board in relation to the appointment of the external auditor and to approve the remuneration and terms of engagement of the external auditor following appointment by the shareholders in general meeting
- to monitor and review the external auditor's independence, objectivity and effectiveness
- to develop and implement policy on the engagement of the external auditor to supply non-audit services.

Where the audit committee's monitoring and review activities reveal cause for concern or scope for improvement, it should make recommendations to the board on action needed to address the issue or to make improvements.

In some cases company management may decide to divide these responsibilities between an audit committee and a risk committee: it would depend on the management's assessment of the need to have one or more committees. The above definition and scope of internal audit points to two key features of internal audit: independence and appraisal.

Even though an internal audit function is normally carried out by the employees of an organisation, it is important that internal auditors enjoy independence from the executives whose work they may audit. Independence is closely related to the fundamental principles of professional conduct as an accountant, in particular to objectivity, professional competence and due care as discussed earlier in Session 1 of this unit. To be effective and independent, the internal auditor's responsibility and authority should be formally established in the organisation's structure, and complemented by the personal competence and professionalism of the internal auditor.

Further, the role of the internal auditor is to *appraise* the work of others involved in the internal control activities rather than actually carrying out those activities. In this sense internal audit provides a service within an organisation rather than implementing any organisational strategies.

Keeping up to date with accounting and auditing developments

You should regularly visit the Auditing Practices Board website, which is accessed through the Financial Reporting Council website at www.frc.org. uk, to follow any future developments in this area for the UK. There are similar websites in other countries.

The websites of professional accounting bodies and major accounting firms are also well worth visiting, as they produce reports and commentaries on auditing issues from time to time. The Financial Reporting Council's website has a useful section devoted to corporate governance. Similar websites may be found for other countries.

4.4.2   Types of internal audit

The previous section showed that the purpose of internal audit is to help achieve effective internal financial and operational control. Internal audit helps to prevent and detect areas of weaknesses in the organisation's financial and operational controls. Depending on what the management of a company may charge the audit function to do, there could be different types and scopes of internal audit. Earlier in this unit you learned about social audit, which involves reviewing and reporting on the impact of organisational activities on society. This is one type of internal audit. Other types include operational audit, systems audit and management investigations into specific aspects of organisational activities. These are discussed below.

Operational audit is concerned with monitoring and reviewing the management's performance against planned benchmarks at different levels in the organisation. The main purpose of operational audits is to evaluate the economy, efficiency and effectiveness of particular operations. That is why operational audits are also known as management, efficiency or value for money audits. Value for money audits are usually carried out in public sector entities and not-for-profit entities.

A systems audit tests or evaluates the internal control processes against benchmark process tests. There are two types of test known as compliance tests and substantive tests. Compliance tests look for evidence that internal controls have been implemented as prescribed by the management. Substantive tests are used to detect any errors and omissions in the financial figures. Figure 2 shows the systems-based audit process. At the compliance test stage the auditor checks for timing, completeness, any omissions or errors and fraudulent entries. If compliance tests show that internal controls are effective then there is less need for substantive testing. If compliance tests reveal evidence of ineffective or less effective internal controls then there is a greater need for substantive tests.

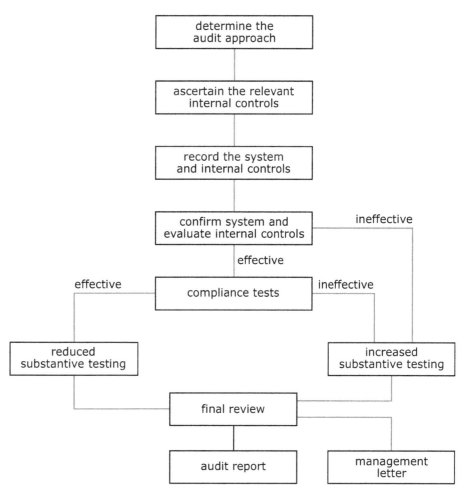

Figure 2 The systems-based audit process

4.4.3 External and internal audit compared

It is essential that you fully understand the differences between an internal audit and an external audit before we proceed any further. Try not to be confused about the roles of the two types of auditor. You need to be aware of how they complement each other and where they diverge. A key difference between internal audit and external audit is the purpose of the two audits. Internal audit is primarily concerned with evaluating management performance and the effectiveness of internal controls, while external audit is primarily concerned with the appraisal of financial statements based on international accounting standards and other relevant legal requirements. Table 3 summarises the major differences.

Table 3 Internal and external audit compared

Area of difference	Internal audit	External audit
Purpose	Appraising management and internal controls	Appraising financial statements
Appointment	By management	By the shareholders (also called members) of the company or the Secretary of State
Relation with organisation	Normally employees, but can be external consultants	Agents
Finance	Internally paid	Paid by fee

Area of difference	Internal audit	External audit
Reporting lines	To management or audit committee	To shareholders (through the audit committee and the management to whom they report)
Legislation	None except in public sector	*Companies Act 2006* and certain other legislation specific to entity audited
Independence	Non-executive	Set by statute
Internal controls	All	Financial and test systems controls
Use of information supplied	To assist management	To examine financial statements
Workload	Continuous review	Usually carries out reviews and looks at the interim financial statements. However, the main auditor report is usually prepared annually
Scope	Determined by management	Set by a statute

The external auditor *may* choose to make use of the internal audit function during the course of the external audit.

'The effective combination of external and internal audit ...'

4.4.4   Evaluating specific internal audit work

The timing of any liaison between the external and internal auditors should be agreed in advance and should be a regular occurrence throughout the audit. If they wish to rely on some of the specific internal audit work for the purpose of the external audit of the financial statements, the external auditors should obtain a sufficient understanding of the internal audit activities to assist them in planning the audit and developing an effective audit approach. This may help in modifying the external audit plan. To do this, the external auditor should assess the internal audit function. In particular, the external auditor is required to consider the internal audit according to the following criteria:

- organisational status
- scope or function

- technical competence
- due professional care.

Activity 4.6

Explain the specific items that you think the external auditor should consider within the criteria identified in Section 4.4.4 immediately preceding this activity. (Spend about ten to fifteen minutes on this activity.)

Feedback

- Organisational status refers to the internal audit's status within the organisation. This status will be granted by management and will influence the ability of the internal auditor to be objective. Traditionally, reporting has been to the finance director but more progressive companies send their internal audit reports to the audit committee in order to increase the objectivity of the internal auditor.
- Scope or function relates to the nature and extent of the assignments that the management allows the internal auditor to perform.
- Technical competence refers to the levels of professional qualification and training required to fulfil the role of an internal auditor.
- Due professional care is the extent to which internal audit work is properly planned, supervised, reviewed and documented.

The use of internal audit work to reduce the overall external audit workload should be evaluated to confirm that it is adequate for external audit purposes. This evaluation of the internal work requires that the following criteria should be considered:

- the work is performed by persons having adequate technical training and proficiency
- the work of assistants is properly supervised, reviewed and documented
- sufficient appropriate audit evidence is obtained to afford a reasonable basis for conclusions reached
- the conclusions reached are appropriate in the circumstances
- any reports prepared by internal audit are consistent with the results of the work performed
- any exceptions or unusual matters disclosed by internal audit are properly resolved
- amendments to the external audit programme are required as a result of matters identified by internal audit work
- there is a need to test the work of internal audit to confirm its adequacy.

Although external auditors may choose to make extensive use of the internal audit function, it is important to remember that they cannot devolve any of their statutory duties. Thus, the external auditor will always retain full responsibility for the audit.

> The external auditor has sole responsibility for the audit opinion expressed, and that responsibility is not reduced by any use made of internal auditing.
>
> ISA 610, p. 2, paragraph 4

Activity 4.7 ....

Do you think that, once internal audit work has been found to be satisfactory, there is no further need to review its work in the future? (Spend no more than five minutes on this activity.)

Feedback ....

No! Internal audit work will need to be reviewed every year by the external auditor to determine whether adequate standards have been maintained.

Summary

In this session you learned how internal audit constitutes an important part of corporate governance. The meaning and scope of internal and external audit was discussed. Internal audit is carried out as part of internal control to ensure that financial statements are in compliance with financial reporting standards and governance codes. However, internal audits of different types can be carried out to prepare a social audit report, an environment audit report, an efficiency or value for money report and a systems audit report.

You also learned about the purpose and scope of an external audit and how this differs from an internal audit. Both internal and external auditors are expected to abide by professional codes of ethics and uphold the fundamental principles of such codes. So far in this unit we have discussed ethics, corporate governance and internal controls, including the role of auditors in the governance mechanisms. One objective of the governance and other mechanisms is to ensure that corporations do their business in a legal and ethical manner. However, there are many cases in the business world where unethical practices and frauds have taken place. In the following session you will learn about fraud prevention and detection.

SESSION **5 Fraud detection and prevention**

Introduction

Fraud in the context of accounting practice can take several forms, but essentially it involves either unlawful misappropriation of assets of an entity or misrepresentation of the facts in financial reporting by the entity. Fraudulent activities in organisations can take place at any level of management. In Sessions 1 and 2 you learned that all employees of an organisation are expected to conduct themselves in an ethical and professional manner so as to secure the assets of the organisation and work in the interests of stakeholders. However, overall responsibility for achieving this lies with the board members who are responsible for putting in place the necessary internal controls and checks to ensure that the entity's assets are safeguarded against various risks, including the risk of fraud. In this session you will learn in more detail about what fraud means and about different types of fraud. The responsibility of an external auditor relating to fraud in an audit of financial statements is also discussed. You will learn about the systems and procedures that may help to detect and prevent fraud.

On completion of Session 5 you are expected to:

- know the meaning of fraud and why fraud happens
- be able to explain the meaning and nature of fraudulent reporting
- be able to explain the meaning and nature of misappropriation of assets
- be able to explain the impact of fraud on stakeholders
- understand fraud detection and prevention mechanisms
- be able to explain the role of auditors with respect to fraud.

5.1 The meaning of fraud

The legal definition of fraud, according to *s.2* of the *Fraud Act 2006* in the UK, is 'dishonestly making a false (untrue or misleading) representation with a view to gain or with intent to cause loss'. However, in a corporate context the meaning is given in definitions of related terms by the Auditing Practices Board. The term fraud is defined as 'an intentional act by one or more individuals among management, those charged with governance, employees, or third parties, involving the use of deception to obtain an unjust or illegal advantage' (APB, 2009b). An intentional act can include statements made by an organisation in its financial reports. Misstatements can arise from either fraud or as a result of an error. The key distinguishing factor between fraud and error is whether the underlying action that results in misstatement of the financial statements is intentional or unintentional.

Two types of intentional misstatement are relevant to the auditor: misstatements resulting from fraudulent financial reporting and misstatements resulting from misappropriation of assets. Fraudulent financial reporting involves intentional misstatements, including omissions of amounts or disclosures in financial statements, to deceive financial statement users. For example, suppose a company receives a very large order for supplying goods to a customer but the order has not yet been fully confirmed. That is, the company is not yet reasonably sure that these sales will be realised. If the company decides to recognise this order as a sale, then it will lead to a false increase in the reported profits for the year.

Misappropriation of assets involves the theft of an entity's assets and is often perpetrated by employees in relatively small and immaterial amounts. However, it can also involve management who are usually more capable of disguising or concealing misappropriations in ways that are difficult to detect. Some examples of accounting-related frauds were reported in the following article from *Forbes* magazine. The article refers to events that occurred in 2001 and 2002 but the descriptions of the allegations illustrate the types of accounting and auditing-related financial frauds that can occur in practice.

The Corporate Scandal Sheet

Penelope Patsuris, 08.26.02

With the avalanche of corporate accounting scandals that have rocked the markets recently, it's getting hard to keep track of them all – but our Corporate Scandal Sheet does the job. Here we'll follow accounting imbroglios only – avoiding insider-trading allegations like those plaguing ImClone, since chronicling every corporate transgression would be impractical – and our timeline starts with the Enron debacle.

Company	When Scandal Went Public	Allegations
Enron	October 2001	Boosted profits and hid debts totalling over $1 billion by improperly using off-the-books partnerships; manipulated the Texas power market; bribed foreign governments to win contracts abroad; manipulated California energy market.
Arthur Andersen	November 2001	Shredding documents related to audit client Enron after the SEC launched an inquiry into Enron.
Homestore.com	January 2002	Inflating sales by booking barter transactions as revenue.
WorldCom	March 2002	Overstated cash flow by booking $3.8 billion in operating expenses as capital expenses; gave founder Bernard Ebbers $400 million in off-the-books loans.
Adelphia Communications	April 2002	Founding Rigas family collected $3.1 billion in off-balance-sheet loans backed by Adelphia; overstated results by inflating capital expenses and hiding debt.
Halliburton	May 2002	Improperly booked $100 million in annual construction cost overruns before customers agreed to pay for them.

Company	When Scandal Went Public	Allegations
AOL Time Warner	July 2002	As the ad market faltered and AOL's purchase of Time Warner loomed, AOL inflated sales by booking barter deals and ads it sold on behalf of others as revenue to keep its growth rate up and seal the deal. AOL also boosted sales via 'round-trip' deals with advertisers and suppliers.
Bristol-Myers Squibb	July 2002	Inflated its 2001 revenue by $1.5 billion by 'channel stuffing,' or forcing wholesalers to accept more inventory than they can sell to get it off the manufacturer's books.
Merck	July 2002	Recorded $12.4 billion in consumer-to-pharmacy co-payments that Merck never collected.

Source: Adapted from 'The corporate scandal sheet' (Patsuris, 2002)

Activity 5.1

In the above article from *Forbes*, underline the accounting and/or auditing-related issues raised by the alleged frauds and list the ones you have noted. (Spend about ten minutes on this activity.)

Feedback

The most common alleged misleading representation in financial statements seems to be inflating the revenues through various ways of accounting or data manipulation. For example, some companies recognised revenues by inflating sales volumes while others recognised advertising revenues based on false sales. Overstatement of assets and liabilities and recognising operating expenses as capital expenditures are some other examples. In the case of Arthur Andersen there is a serious violation of the standard audit practice of obtaining and keeping evidence. In this case, Arthur Andersen destroyed audit-related documents for Enron, which was its audit client, when inquiry into Enron activities was announced in the USA.

5.2 Why does fraud take place?

Around the world corporate frauds and scandals have taken place. Misstatement of financial statements has been quite common in many such frauds. Three common characteristics of fraud are:

- incentive or pressure to commit fraud
- a perceived opportunity to do so
- individual characteristics in the fraudster that allow such a person to rationalise fraudulent behaviour.

Perhaps the most important thing facilitating the occurrence of fraud is human willingness to engage in such an act intentionally. An honest individual generally will not commit fraud even if there is an incentive or an opportunity to do so.

An incentive could arise from pressure on management to achieve performance targets. These could be factors external or internal to the organisation. For example, the management of a company may be tempted to report inflated earnings with the intention of influencing the share price of the company. In another situation, the senior management's compensation package may depend on a share price increase or on an increase in reported earnings per share, creating an incentive for managers to indulge in manipulation of earnings by changing accounting policies or by misreporting losses. Individuals may also misappropriate assets such as inventory, cash or other easily transported assets. Opportunities for fraud also arise when internal checks and controls are inadequate. This may happen when, for example, expense reimbursement procedures are not robust or a person in a position of trust, say, a warehouse manager, abuses that position and allows misappropriation of assets. However, as pointed out earlier, the primary requisite for fraud must be that individuals are willing to compromise on ethics and personal integrity.

5.3 Fraudulent financial reporting

Much of the discussion here on fraudulent reporting and auditors' responsibility and procedures draws on ISA 330 and ISA 240. ISA 330 relates to an auditor's procedures in response to assessed risks and ISA 240 describes an auditor's responsibilities relating to fraud in the audit of financial statement.

According to ISA 330 (UK and Ireland) fraudulent financial reporting involves intentional misstatements, including omissions of amounts or disclosures in financial statements, to deceive financial statement users. It can be caused by the efforts of management to manage earnings in order to deceive financial statement users by influencing their perceptions about the entity's performance and profitability. For such earnings management may start out with small actions or inappropriate adjustment of assumptions and changes in judgements. Pressures and incentives may increase these actions to the extent that they result in fraudulent financial reporting. Such a situation could occur when, owing to pressures to meet market expectations or a desire to maximise compensation based on performance, management intentionally take actions that lead to fraudulent financial reporting, by materially misstating the financial statements. In some entities, management may be motivated to reduce earnings by a material amount to minimise tax or to inflate earnings to secure bank financing.

Listed below are some of the ways in which fraudulent reporting may be carried out. Often there is not a single method. It may be worth recalling the post-closing trial balance adjustments or end of period adjustments that you learned in Unit 4, as you will find below some methods that abuse that accounting adjustment process. Note also that fraudulent financial reporting often involves overriding internal controls.

1   Manipulation, falsification (including forgery), or alteration of accounting records or supporting documentation from which the financial statements are prepared. Examples of such fraudulent activities include payroll frauds where false timesheets may be prepared to claim wages or where fictitious members of staff are created to allow fraudsters to steal money from the business. A real example of the latter type emerged in the case of the Satyam company, where an inquiry into the largest accounting-related fraud in India showed that thousands of fictitious

employee contracts were created and salaries drawn in those names. More details about this corporate fraud are provided in the case study later in this session.

2   Misrepresentation in, or intentional omission from, the financial statements of events, transactions or other significant information.

3   Intentional misapplication of accounting principles relating to amounts, classification, manner of presentation or disclosure.

4   Recording fictitious journal entries, particularly close to the end of an accounting period, to manipulate operating results or achieve other objectives.

5   Inappropriately adjusting assumptions and changing judgements used to estimate account balances.

6   Omitting, advancing or delaying recognition in the financial statements of events and transactions that have occurred during the reporting period. An example of this could be not recognising irrecoverable receivables when it would have been prudent to do so but continuing to show such receivables as assets. The consequence of such actions will be overstatement of the profits.

7   Concealing, or not disclosing, facts that could affect the amounts recorded in the financial statements.

8   Altering records and terms related to significant and unusual transactions.

Fraudsters could potentially abuse the computerised accounting and information systems, resulting in fraudulent reporting or misappropriation of assets. The threat of fraud arising from breach of computer security systems is one of the biggest risks faced by most business entities.

Activity 5.2 ....

Can you think of any situation where you have witnessed an accounting fraud or have been a victim of a fraud? Which of the types mentioned above do you think was most relevant to the situation which you experienced? (Spend no more than ten minutes on this activity.)

There is no feedback for this activity, but you may reflect on the situation on your own and perhaps share your thoughts with fellow students through the forums provided on the B291 website.

5.4 Misappropriation of assets

Assets of a business may be misappropriated in many ways and may involve management who are usually able to disguise or conceal misappropriations in ways that are difficult to detect. Misappropriation of assets is often accompanied by false or misleading records or documents in order to conceal the fact that the assets are missing or have been pledged without proper authorisation. Misappropriation of assets can be accomplished in a variety of ways including:

1   embezzling receipts (for example, misappropriating collections on accounts receivable or diverting receipts in respect of written-off accounts to personal bank accounts)

2   stealing physical assets or intellectual property (for example, stealing inventory for personal use or for sale, stealing scrap for resale, or colluding with a competitor by disclosing technological data in return for payment)

3   causing an entity to pay for goods and services not received (for example, payments to fictitious vendors, 'kickbacks' paid by vendors to the entity's purchasing agents in return for inflating prices, payments to fictitious employees, etc.)

4   using an entity's assets for personal use (for example, using the entity's assets as collateral for a personal loan or a loan to a related party).

'Frankly, Mr Clause, we don't understand – two days ago you had assets worth billions – today, nothing...'

5.5   Impact of fraud

The impact of fraud on any organisation will depend on the type of fraud that has been carried out. One way to understand the impact is to consider the implications for different stakeholders in the organisation. If a financial reporting fraud resulted in understatement of profits, the share price might fall and net profits available for distribution to shareholders as dividends will fall. Understatement of profits will also affect the tax payable, which will be a loss to the government. Fraudulent activities resulting in an overstatement of profits, say, an over-estimate of the closing inventory, may result in higher reported earnings. This in turn may create an impression of better company performance than is actually achieved. This may also impact on the bonuses payable to management if their performance is linked to reported earnings. Overstated profits may also impact on suppliers' or on bankers' perceptions of the risks involved in dealing with a company.

A fraud involving embezzlement of cash or misappropriation of assets is a direct loss to the owners of the business. A fraud involving manipulation of records reduces the reliability of the financial reports thereby increasing the perception of risk about the company. There could also be a reputation loss. These implications may make it difficult for current and potential investors to value the company properly.

Fraudulent activities involving inadequate provision for pension liabilities may affect the future pension receipts of the employees retiring from the company. The implications of big corporate frauds may undermine the confidence of public and prospective investors not only in the company concerned but also in the industry sector as a whole. The implications of fraud thus could have an effect on a wider group of stakeholders in business than just the immediately obvious one.

5.6 Detecting and preventing fraud

Corporate governance codes in most countries make it very clear that the overall responsibility for detecting and preventing fraud lies with senior managers and the board of directors. As was discussed earlier in this unit, the scope of internal controls includes the need for effective mechanisms within an organisation at all levels to detect and prevent fraud. The risk of fraud is an important risk that needs to be understood by all managers and accountants. The management must assess the risk to the company as befits the size, complexity and nature of the business. Therefore, the nature and frequency of assessment of the risk of fraud will vary from business to business. In smaller entities the risks might lie more in the misappropriation of assets than in fraudulent reporting. It is, however, necessary that business entities have systematic procedures, incentives and policies that support fraud detection and prevention.

Formal fraud detection and prevention procedures are usually part of wider internal control systems and risk management functions. However, it is desirable that all the employees of an entity be made aware of policies to decrease the chance of fraud. This may involve formal training and awareness-raising programmes whereby employees are shown where and how fraud might take place so that they can exercise effective monitoring. Detection of fraud may be improved by internal checks or by identifying and segregating staff duties in key control areas, such as approving purchase orders or monitoring operational controls. Some other ways to reduce the chances of fraud include appropriate documentation, providing guidelines on purchases from specified suppliers, and appropriate hierarchy of access to databases or computerised dealings with suppliers, customers and bankers. An effective internal control system to prevent fraud may have one or more of the following features. Note, though, that this is not an exhaustive list of preventative mechanisms, as by its very nature fraudulent action may use different techniques to circumvent any fraud prevention mechanisms.

1   *Physical controls.* Misappropriation of assets, such as theft of petty cash or inventory, could be prevented by putting in place appropriate physical controls, which may range from keeping

cash in a lockable box to electronic surveillance. The access to physical assets could be controlled by allowing only authorised staff to enter the related space. Frequently these days there are multiple layers of preventative mechanisms. Consider an office where a cash box is kept. The entry to the office could be monitored through a closed circuit TV camera, the access to the office could be restricted and monitored through the use of an electronic card, and the cash box itself could have a digital or physical lock. Physical controls are thus the most common and perhaps the most essential requirement for prevention of fraud.

2 *Separation of duties*. Many business activities involve a set of tasks and documents related to those tasks. For example, the purchase of materials may involve requisition from a production department, and the purchase manager may decide the quantity to be ordered and the supplier from whom to source that material. He or she may be involved in the receipt of materials and checking the inventory received, raising a pay order or payment authorisation, and in payment to the supplier. To prevent fraud it may be desirable to separate the duties so that the person requisitioning is not the same as the person authorising and so on. Such controls could be useful in many other functions of the business.

3 *Authorisation policies*. Requiring formal authorisation from a senior manager for large orders, deliveries or payments may be a good preventative mechanism as it puts in place the additional oversight of large transactions.

4 *Documentary details*. In Units 2 and 4 you learned about various sources of data from which accounting information is generated. You may have noticed many details recorded on those documents. These recorded details can help prevent frauds. For example, getting a customer signature on a despatch note on receipt of goods delivered is a commonly used fraud prevention mechanism. The signature ensures that the quantity and quality of goods delivered were as per the customer's order. For the business it becomes evidence that the customer received the goods.

5 *Managerial responsibilities in fraud detection and prevention*. Risk of fraud taking place exists right from the top of the management structure to the lowest levels of management hierarchy. Therefore, it is important that those charged with governance ensure that all members of the organisation are made aware of their roles in the prevention and detection of fraud. The board of directors must ensure that there is an appropriate policy for assessing the risk of fraud and that the policy is implemented. This is usually done by creating and empowering an internal audit and risk committee, as was discussed earlier in the unit. Non-executive directors on the board are responsible for scrutinising the decisions by the executive directors. If non-executive directors detect or suspect any fraud by board members or senior managers, they should raise the matter in board meetings and/or inform the relevant board level committee, such as the internal audit committee.

All operational managers should be alert to the possibility of fraud and must exercise their duties of monitoring the staff and the functions supervised by them. For example, a sales manager should be alert to receiving unusually large or small orders from one region or one client. A finance manager should look for unusual items or trends in accounting data. The role of internal auditors includes scrutinising financial records to detect any potential fraud when they carry out operational audit or efficiency audits, as discussed in Session 4.

It was discussed earlier that a key requirement for a fraud to take place is an individual's willingness to compromise on ethical principles and personal integrity. Alternatively, an individual's willingness to uphold ethical principles and values may help to prevent fraud. Some honest employees may decide to make the management aware of any fraud they may detect. Honest employees must be protected against any disciplinary action or other consequences so that they are not discouraged from reporting any fraud in the company.

5.7 Role of auditors with respect to fraud detection

Much of the foregoing discussion of financial frauds is based on ISA 240 (UK and Ireland), which also sets out the auditor's responsibility relating to fraud in the audit of financial statements. Since expressing an opinion about the truth and fairness of financial statements is a key responsibility of an auditor, the International Standards on Auditing make it clear that the primary responsibility for the prevention and detection of fraud in the context of financial reporting rests with those responsible for the governance of an entity, and its management. So far as the responsibility of the auditor is concerned, ISA 240 (2009) says that 'an auditor conducting an audit in accordance with ISAs (UK and Ireland) is responsible for obtaining reasonable assurance that the financial statements taken as a whole are free from material misstatement, whether caused by fraud or error' (p. 3, paragraph 5). Owing to the inherent limitations of an audit, there is an unavoidable risk that some material misstatements in the financial statements may not be detected, even though the audit is properly planned and performed in accordance with the ISAs (UK and Ireland).

However, the ISA further says that:

> When obtaining reasonable assurance, the auditor is responsible for maintaining professional scepticism throughout the audit, considering the potential for management override of controls and recognising the fact that audit procedures that are effective for detecting error may not be effective in detecting fraud.
>
> ISA 240, p. 4, paragraph 8

The ISA lays down the following objectives for the auditor with respect to fraud during the auditing process:

(a) to identify and assess the risks of material misstatement of the financial statements due to fraud

(b) to obtain sufficient appropriate audit evidence regarding the assessed risks of material misstatement due to fraud, through designing and implementing appropriate responses

(c) to respond appropriately to fraud or suspected fraud identified during the audit.

> ISA 240, p. 4, paragraph 10

If the auditors, after undertaking appropriate risk assessment procedures, consider that one or more fraud risk factors are present, they should design and perform further audit procedures as necessary. Fraud risk factors include events or conditions that indicate an incentive or pressure to commit fraud or provide an opportunity to commit fraud. In other words, the auditors should include an explicit consideration of the risk of fraud as part of their audit planning procedures.

So far we have discussed various ways in which fraud can take place. Let us conclude this session with a dramatic corporate scandal that temporarily shook the confidence stock markets had in India's IT industry and caused a lot of concern about the professional behaviour of auditors.

In early 2009 the chairman of one of the largest IT companies in India declared that he had been involved in one of the largest accounting frauds in the world and the largest fraud to date in India. The scale and complexity of the fraud was so huge that continuing the concealment of fraudulent activities became impossible, forcing the chairman to declare what was going on. He did this in a letter of resignation, which is reproduced in part below.

Letter of resignation written by Mr B.R. Raju, Chairman, to the Satyam Board

It is with deep regret and tremendous burden that I am carrying on my conscience, that I would like to bring the following facts to your notice:

1   The Balance Sheet carries as of September 30, 2008,

One crore rupees (Rs) = 10 million Indian rupees (Rs)

    a) Inflated (non-existent) cash and bank balances of Rs 5,040 crore (as against Rs 5,361 crore reflected in the books);

    b) An accrued interest of Rs 376 crore, which is non-existent

    c) An understated liability of Rs 1,230 crore on account of funds arranged by me;

    d) An overstated debtors' position of Rs 490 crore (as against Rs 2,651 reflected in the books);

2   For the September quarter (Q2) we reported a revenue of Rs 2,700 crore and an operating margin of Rs 649 crore (24 per cent of revenue) as against the actual revenues of Rs 2,112 crore and an actual operating margin of Rs 61 crore (3 per cent of revenues). This has resulted in artificial cash and bank balances going up by Rs 588 crore in Q2 alone.

The gap in the balance sheet has arisen purely on account of inflated profits over several years (limited only to Satyam books of subsidiaries reflecting true performance).

What started as a marginal gap between actual operating profit and the one reflected in the books of accounts continued to grow over the years.

It has attained unmanageable proportions as the size of the company operations grew significantly (annualised revenue run[1] rate of Rs 11,276 crore in the September quarter, 2008, and official reserves of Rs 8,392 crore).

The differential in the real profits and the one reflected in the books was further accentuated by the fact that the company had to carry additional resources and assets to justify a higher level of operations thereby significantly increasing the costs.

---

[1] The language and some terms used in this letter are reproduced exactly as in the letter. Revenue run rate probably means the total revenue or turnover of the company.

Every attempt made to eliminate the gap failed. As the promoters held a small percentage of equity, the concern was that poor performance would result in takeover, thereby exposing the gap. It was like riding a tiger, not knowing how to get off without being eaten.

The aborted Maytas acquisition deal was the last attempt to fill the fictitious assets with real ones. Maytas' investors were convinced that this is a good divestment opportunity and a strategic fit.

Once Satyam's problem was solved, it was hoped that Maytas' payments can be delayed. But that was not to be. What followed in the last several days is common knowledge.

I would like the board to know:

1   That neither myself, nor the Managing Director (including our spouses) sold any shares in the last eight years – excepting for a small proportion declared and sold for philanthropic purposes.

2   That in the last two years a net amount of Rs 1,230 crore was arranged to Satyam (not reflected in the books of Satyam) to keep the operations going by resorting to pledging all the promoter shares and raising funds from known sources by giving all kinds of assurances (statement enclosed only to the members of the board).

   Significant dividend payments, acquisitions, capital expenditure to provide for growth did not help matters. Every attempt was made to keep the wheel moving and to ensure prompt payment of salaries to the associates. The last straw was the selling of most of the pledged shares by the lenders on account of margin triggers.[2]

3   That neither me nor the managing director took even one rupee/dollar from the company and have not benefited in financial terms on account of the inflated results.

4   None of the board members, past or present, had any knowledge of the situation in which the company is placed.

   ...

Having put these facts before you, I leave it to the wisdom of the board to take the matters forward.

...

Under the circumstances, I am tendering the resignation as the chairman of Satyam and shall continue in this position only till such time the current board is expanded. My continuance is just to ensure enhancement of the board over the next several days or as early as possible.

I am now prepared to subject myself to the laws of the land and face the consequences thereof.

(B Ramalinga Raju)

Copies marked to:

1   Chairman SEBI [Securities Exchange Board of India]
2   Stock Exchanges.

Source: *The Financial Express* (2009)

Activity 5.3 ....

1   Based on your reading of the Satyam Chairman's letter, what do you think seems to be origin of the fraudulent reporting?
2   What is the nature of the fraudulent activity in this case?

(Spend no more than 15 minutes on this activity.)

---

[2] Margin is a technical term used in the trading of financial securities, which broadly means the deposit requirement to be made by the buyer or seller of securities. Margin is usually a percentage of the value of the outstanding value of securities bought or sold by participants in the financial markets.

Feedback

1   There is an indication in the letter that the whole thing started with a desire to show better than actual profits in some financial year in the past but it grew out of control. This could have been driven by either a desire to meet forecast profit targets or for some other reason: it is not clear.

2   This is a case of fraudulent misstatement of almost all accounting elements: revenues, expenses, assets and liabilities. This is borne out by overstatement and understatement of various items. There are even fictitious assets such as bank balances. Questions can be asked about the efficacy of internal control systems in this company.

Subsequently, enquiries were held and Mr Raju was arrested, but the case is not yet over at the time of writing of this unit. However, investigations by the Central Bureau of Investigation (CBI) in India have revealed some of the ways in which this fraud was carried out. These are reported in an article that was published in *Accountancy Age* and is reproduced below.

Satyam fraud methodology revealed

The Central Bureau of Investigation (CBI) of India has revealed details of the fake invoicing system used by Satyam Computer Services Ltd as part of the US$1 billion-plus fraud that has rocked the company.

Documents released to the general public in India showed how the company's standard billing systems were subverted to generate 'false invoices to show inflated sales,' before its former boss Ramalinga Raju admitted his role in India's largest ever corporate scandal.

The CBI said it had used cyber-forensics to uncover how in-house computer systems were exploited to generate fake invoices.

Regular Satyam bills were created by a computer application called 'Operational Real Time Management (OPTIMA)', which creates and maintains information on company projects. The 'Satyam Project Repository (SRP)' system then generates project IDs; there is also an 'Ontime' application for entering the hours worked by Satyam employees; and a 'Project Bill Management System (PBMS)' for billing. An 'Invoice Management System (IMS)' generated the final invoices.

CBI officers have concluded that the scandal involved this system structure being bypassed by the abuse of an emergency 'Excel Porting' system, which allows 'invoices [to] be generated directly in IMS ... by porting the data into the IMS.' This system was subverted by the creation of a user ID called 'Super User' with 'the power to hide/unhide the invoices generated in IMS'.

By 'logging in as a Super User, the accused were hiding some of the invoices that were generated through Excel Porting. Once an invoice is hidden the same will not be visible to the other divisions within the company but will only be visible to the [company's finance division sales team]' concluded the CBI.

As a result, 'concerned business circles' would not be aware of the invoices, which were 'also not dispatched to the customers'. The note added: 'Investigation revealed that all the invoices that were hidden using the Super User ID in the IMS server were found to be false and fabricated.' The value of these fake invoices 'were shown as receivables in the books of accounts of [Satyam] thereby dishonestly inflating the revenues of the company.'

And there were a lot of these bills. The CBI said their inquiries revealed there are 7,561 invoices found hidden in the invoice management system, worth INDRupees 51 billion (US$1.01 billion). 'As a result of this analysis, the individuals who have generated and hidden these false and fabricated invoices have been identified,' said the law enforcement agency.

Source: Verma, R. and Nuthall, K. (2009) *Accountancy Age*, 29 Apr 2009

Activity 5.4   ....

Do you find that any of the methods used by Satyam are similar to those described in this unit? What factors created such an opportunity for the fraud to take place? (Spend no more than 15 minutes on this activity.)

Feedback   ....

Several of the methods described in Section 5.3 are used in this case. The opportunity for such fraud was created by completely automated accounting systems and the use of a computerised payments and receipts system. This itself would not have been a problem if the internal controls had not been overridden. You may recall that earlier in this unit you learned that frequently in fraudulent action management overrides the internal procedures and checks to prevent fraud, which in this case seems to have happened – and right at the highest level of the organisation. Clearly there is no protection against fraud if the most senior managers decide to compromise on their personal integrity and ethics.

Summary

In this session you learned about the meaning of fraud in an accounting context. It was emphasised that three conditions allow fraud to take place:

1   there have to be incentives or pressures on individuals or a group in the organisation to engage intentionally in fraudulent action
2   there has to be an opportunity for engaging in such action
3   the person or persons involved have to be willing to compromise on their ethical principles and personal integrity.

Fraudulent reporting and fraudulent misappropriation of assets were explained as two main types of fraud. The specific nature of various types of fraudulent reporting and misappropriation were discussed. The session also discussed the role of internal and external auditors in fraud prevention and detection. Various ways of fraud prevention and detection were described and illustrated with examples of corporate scandals.

Eric & Bill

10/17

'I took a course in ethics, but everything was contradicted by the course I took in *accounting*.'

Unit summary

This unit started with the following learning outcomes and aims to enable you to:

- understand and discuss ethics and professional values in the context of accounting
- explain the need to comply with ethical, professional and regulatory frameworks
- discuss the need for and the scope of corporate governance
- explain the relationship between ethics, governance, the law and social responsibility
- explain the role and functions of internal and external auditing
- explain the need for and process of preventing accounting-related fraud.

In **Session 1** you learned about the meaning of and the need for ethical considerations in business and accounting contexts. It was noted that ethical dilemmas could be difficult to resolve in real life but in an accounting context a conceptual framework was available that could be used to deal with ethical dilemmas. A key learning point from this session is that an accountant is a professional and needs to abide by a professional code of ethics that upholds the fundamental principles of integrity, objectivity, independence, professional competence, due care and confidentiality.

Session 2 covered the need for corporate governance and its scope. Corporate governance as a set of mechanisms to reduce the agency problem and to make management of companies accountable to various stakeholders was discussed. You learned about the meaning of and the difference between the rules-based and the principles-based approaches to corporate governance. The principles-based approach to corporate governance was illustrated by explaining the elements of corporate governance enshrined in the *Combined Code on Corporate Governance* in the UK. A distinguishing feature of a rules-based approach is its legally binding compliance as opposed to a principles-based approach that implements recommended best practice.

Session 3 brought together the discussion of ethics, corporate governance, law and the concept of corporate social responsibility. Corporate social responsibility as a concept is relatively new, although it has acquired considerable significance in corporate activities as many large companies now support social, economic and environmental activities to meet the expectations that society has of business. You learned that CSR was about going beyond ethical, legal and governance expectations. It was discussed that in real life CSR reporting overlaps with social and environmental reports.

In **Session 4** internal and external audit were discussed in the context of internal control. Internal control was discussed in detail as an important element of corporate governance. You learned how an entity may create a control environment by putting in place policies and structures to implement internal control. Internal audit was discussed as an independent appraisal of internal financial controls to ensure that an entity complies with relevant reporting standards and governance codes. The external auditor's role with respect to internal audit and the auditing of financial statements was discussed in this session. It was emphasised that auditors have to abide by professional standards and must act in the public interest, which was also mentioned in Session 1 of the unit.

Finally, **Session 5** explained the meaning of fraud. The difference between fraud and error was explained by the presence of an intention to misstate or misappropriate, in the case of fraud. Fraudulent financial reporting and misappropriation of assets from the company were discussed as two main types of fraud. Various ways in which fraud can take place and various preventative mechanisms to reduce fraud were discussed in the session. The session ended with a case study of a real life accounting reporting fraud.

A central theme of this unit has been that the board of directors and senior managers have fiduciary responsibilities to manage the business in the interests of various stakeholders. How the board prioritises the interests of different stakeholders may depend on the corporate governance environment in which the company operates, such as in the UK (shareholder-oriented) or in Germany (wider stakeholder perspective). In this overall context, the role of the professional accountant is crucial as he/she may prepare financial reports, may be an internal or external auditor, or may occupy a management role in a company.

In the final unit you will learn about some of the UK laws that are relevant in a business and accounting context. The unit will also provide a concluding summary of the entire module.

Self-assessed Questions

Question 1

One of the common financial reporting scandals relates to companies overstating profits through various ways of recognising revenues or under-estimating expenses. Read the following article about one of the many accounting scandals that have taken place in recent corporate history. Then:

(a) identify and comment on accounting principles involved in the errors

(b) identify and comment on any corporate governance failures in this case.

WorldCom accounting scandal

WorldCom has revealed a further $3.3bn in accounting errors, doubling the size of the accounting scandal at America's second largest long distance phone company to more than $7bn. Mark Tran explains.

The company said an internal audit had discovered that $3.3bn in profits were improperly recorded on its books from 1999 to the first quarter of 2002. That is on top of the $3.8bn in expenses the company said it had improperly reported as capital investments. WorldCom now says it must issue revised financial statements for 2000 and 1999 as well. The revision will reduce 2000 profits by more than $3.2bn, but this may not be the end of accounting horrors as the company warned it may find more problems.

WorldCom said most of the $3.3bn irregularity involved the manipulation of reserves. Companies set aside reserves to cover estimated losses such as uncollected payments from customers and judgements in lawsuits and other expected costs.

It is a perfectly legitimate practice, like setting aside funds for a rainy day. But reserves can be abused to create the accounting equivalent of a slush fund. If a company wanted to massage profits to meet Wall Street expectations it can transfer the necessary sums from the reserve. The suspicion is that WorldCom deliberately inflated its reserves to be able to dip into them to boost profits in order to meet profit projections.

WorldCom's chief executive, John Sidgmore, blamed the company's former chief financial officer, Scott Sullivan, and the former controller, David Myers. The two were fired for claiming $3.8bn in regular expenses as capital investment in 2001. The pair were arrested in New York, handcuffed and paraded in front of TV cameras as part of the Bush's administration crackdown on corporate crime. Charged with securities fraud, conspiracy and other charges, they face 65 years in prison. WorldCom's founder and former chief executive, Bernie Ebbers, says he was unaware of the accounting problems, and has not been charged.

Operating expenses must be subtracted from revenue immediately, while the cost of capital expenses can be spread over time. Improperly spreading operating costs inflated WorldCom's profits.

WorldCom's accountants at the time were Arthur Andersen, the same people that looked after Enron's books as well as other companies hit by accounting issues – Tyco, Global Crossing and Adelphia. Andersen accused Mr Sullivan of withholding information from them. The deputy US attorney general, Larry Thompson, said: 'We have to ask where the professionals were, the accountants and the lawyers.'

WorldCom has new accountants, KPMG, who have been asked to scour the books back to 1999. It will be virtually impossible to get an accurate picture until a comprehensive audit for the past several years is done, a process expected to last months. The company is also under investigation by the department of justice and the securities and exchange commission, the US financial regulator. WorldCom, which has been charged with fraud for allegedly hiding $1.2bn in losses, is now under bankruptcy protection.

WorldCom said it may have to write off $50bn when it restates its finances. One of the largest write-offs in corporate history, that would amount to the 2001 gross domestic products of Hungary and the Czech Republic. Only Time Warner's $54bn write-off was bigger.

Source: Tran, M. (2002), *The Guardian*, 9 August 2002

Suggested answer

(a) *Accounting principles involved*

The company under-estimated the recurring expenses by capitalising them. This violates the prudence and matching principles. This resulted in misstatement of the profits for the period of 1999–2003. There appears to have been a tendency to resort to accounting manipulation to report profits higher than those that would have been appropriate had all expenses been recognised according to accounting principles.

(b) *Corporate governance failures*

There appears to be an internal audit function in the company but it either failed to detect accounting irregularity in terms of treating operating expenses as capital expenditure or the internal audit noticed it but did not report it to the board. One may wonder whether the board would have taken action if the irregularity had been reported to it. There is also the failure by external auditors in not collecting adequate evidence as part of the audit to ascertain the nature of the operating expenses that were charged as capital expenditure. It is not clear when Arthur Andersen knew that the Chief Financial Officer was withholding information from them. It is reported that the Chief Executive Officer did not know about accounting irregularities and was therefore not charged with financial crime. However, this case relates to 2002. A similar argument now perhaps will not protect a CEO in the USA as the *Sarbanes–Oxley Act 2002* requires that the CEO certify the accuracy of financial statements.

Question 2 ....

Briefly describe the importance of remuneration policy for directors and senior executives from a corporate governance perspective.

Suggested answer ....

As long-term success of the company is a key objective of corporate governance, it must ensure that the interests of the directors of the company are aligned with the key stakeholders, particularly the shareholders. For this to happen, the remuneration policy is used to attract, retain and motivate the directors and other senior managers. Linking of remuneration to the key performance measures needed to achieve the corporate objectives leads to alignment of the interests of shareholders and the directors. Thus an effective remuneration policy may help reduce the agency problem and improve effectiveness of corporate governance.

Question 3 ....

What is the role of non-executive directors in corporate governance?

Suggested answer ....

Non-executive directors are expected to play an important role in the effectiveness of corporate governance. According to the UK Combined Code the non-executive directors as independent directors are supposed to scrutinise the decisions of the most senior management and challenge their assumptions and behaviour with a view to improving overall management effectiveness. Usually some important committees such as the Audit Committee, Risk Committee and Remuneration Committee are chaired by the non-executive directors.

Question 4 ....

Briefly describe the five fundamental principles of the professional code of ethics for accountants.

Suggested answer ....

The International Federation of Accountants sets out the following five fundamental principles of the professional code of ethics for accountants.

1   *Integrity*: a professional accountant should be straightforward and honest in all professional and business relationships.

2   *Objectivity*: a professional accountant should not allow bias, conflict of interest or undue influence of others to override professional or business judgments.

3   *Professional competence and due care*: a professional accountant has a continuing duty to maintain professional knowledge and skill at the level required to ensure that a client or employer receives competent professional service based on current developments in practice, legislation and techniques. A professional accountant should act diligently and in accordance with applicable technical and professional standards when providing professional services.

4   *Confidentiality*: a professional accountant should respect the confidentiality of information acquired as a result of professional and business relationships and should not disclose any such information to third parties without proper and specific authority unless there is a legal or professional right or duty to disclose. Confidential information acquired as a result of professional and business relationships should not be used for the personal advantage of the professional accountant or third parties.

5   *Professional behaviour*: a professional accountant should comply with relevant laws and regulations and should avoid any action that discredits the profession.

Question 5

On the B291 website you will find a pdf file containing the external auditor's report for the French company EDF (see p. 134 of the pdf).

After reading the auditor's report respond to the following questions:

1   Does EDF follow International Financial Reporting Standards in preparing its financial statements?

2   On which matters have the auditors expressed different opinions without qualifying their report?

Suggested answer

1   Yes, according to the auditor's report, EDF follows IFRS as adopted by the European Union.

2   The auditors have pointed out that the expected gains from the nuclear electricity business of the company are subject to many assumptions. According to the auditors, valuation of long term provisions are sensitive to the assumptions made concerning costs, inflation rates, long term discount rates (where 'discount rate' is a required return on capital that companies use in evaluating projects), and forecast cash flows.

The auditors also seem to suggest that providing for replacement of assets using a different approach (discounted value of future payments) will lead to a material difference in the estimates of replacement costs.

This report illustrates the issue of judgement, alluded to in this unit, which is involved in accounting policy decisions.

References

Table of statutes and statutory instruments

Great Britain. *Building Societies Act 1986. Elizabeth II. Chapter 53.* (1986) London: The Stationery Office.

Great Britain. *Companies Act 2006. Elizabeth II. Chapter 46.* (2006) London: The Stationery Office.

Great Britain. *Financial Services and Markets Act 2000. Elizabeth II. Chapter 8.* (2000) London: The Stationery Office.

Great Britain. *Trade Union and Labour Relations (Consolidation) Act 1992. Elizabeth II. Chapter 52.* (1992) London: The Stationery Office.

The Companies Act 2006 (Amendment) (Accounts and Reports) Regulations 2008 (SI 2008/393).

United States of America. *Sarbanes–Oxley Act (SOX) 2002.* Public Law 107–204 (2002). 107th Congress. The Senate and House of Representatives of the United States of America.

Publications

Auditing Practices Board (2008) *APB Ethical Standard 5 (Revised): Non-Audit Services Provided to Audited Entities*; London, Auditing Practices Board; also available online at http://www.frc.org.uk/apb/publications/pub1569.html (accessed 7 May 2010).

Auditing Practices Board (2009a) *A UK Publicly Traded Company* [online], http://www.frc.org.uk/apb/scope/UKP.cfm (accessed 1 September 2010).

Auditing Practices Board (2009b) *Glossary of Terms*, London, Auditing Practices Board; also available at http://www.frc.org.uk/images/uploaded/documents/Glossary%20of%20Terms.pdf (accessed 13 March 2010).

Berle Jr, A.A. and Means, G.C. (1933) *The Modern Corporation and Private Property*, New York, NY, Macmillan Co.

Black, J., Hashimzade, N. and Myles, G. (2009) *A Dictionary of Economics*, Oxford, Oxford University Press; also available online at http://www.oxfordreference.com/views/ENTRY.html?subview=Main&entry=t19.e302 (accessed 3 April 2009).

Cadbury Committee (1992) 'Cadbury Report' (full title: *The Financial Aspects of Corporate Governance*), London, Gee; also available online at http://www.ecgi.org/codes/documents/cadbury.pdf (accessed 14 October 2010).

Carroll, A.B. (1991) 'The pyramid of corporate social responsibility: toward the moral management of organizational stakeholders', *Business Horizons*, vol. 34, no. 4, pp. 39–48.

Combined Code on Corporate Governance (2008), London, Financial Reporting Council.

Committee on Basic Auditing Concepts (1969–71), *Accounting Review*, 1972 Supplement, vol. 47, no. 4, p. 18.

De La Rue (2009) 'Business Review: Risk and Risk Management', *Annual Report 2009*, Basingstoke, De La Rue.

Drucker, P. (1954) *The Practice of Management*, London, Butterworth-Heinemann.

Drucker, P. (2002a) *Managing in a Time of Great Change*, Oxford, Butterworth-Heinemann.

Drucker, P. (2002b) *A Functioning Society: Selections from Sixty-five Years of Writing on Community, Society and Polity*, New Brunswick, NJ, Transaction.

European Commission (undated) 'Sustainable and responsible business: corporate social responsibility (CSR)', *Enterprise and Industry* [online], http://ec.europa.eu/enterprise/csr/campaign/index_en.htm (accessed 7 October 2009).

Fairtrade Foundation (2010) *FAQs* [online], http://www.fairtrade.org.uk/what_is_fairtrade/faqs.aspx (accessed 25 August 2010).

Financial Reporting Council (2010) *True and Fair* [online], http://www.frc.org.uk/about/trueandfair.cfm (accessed 1 September 2010).

Freeman, E. (1984) *Strategic Management: A Stakeholder Perspective,* Boston, Pitman.

Institute of Chartered Accountants in England and Wales (2009) *Members' Handbook*, London, Institute of Chartered Accountants.

Institute of Internal Auditors (2010) *Definition of Internal Auditing* [online], http://www.theiia.org/guidance/standards-and-guidance/ippf/definition-of-internal-auditing/ (accessed 1 September 2010).

International Ethics Standards Board for Accountants (2012) *Handbook of the Code of Ethics for Professional Accountants*, New York, NY, International Federation of Accountants.

International Federation of Accountants (2005) *Code of Ethics for Professional Accountants*, New York, NY, International Federation of Accountants.

International Federation of Accountants (2009) *Code of Ethics for Professional Accountants*, New York, NY, International Federation of Accountants.

International Standard on Auditing (UK and Ireland) 240 (2009), 'The auditor's responsibilities relating to fraud in an audit of financial statements', Financial Reporting Council, available online from http://www.frc.org.uk/apb/publications/pub2080.html (accessed 1 November 2010).

International Standard on Auditing (UK and Ireland) (ISA (UK and Ireland)) 315 (2004), 'Understanding the entity and its environment and assessing the risks of material misstatement', Financial Reporting Council, available online from http://www.frc.org.uk/images/uploaded/documents/ACF15D.pdf (accessed 1 November 2010).

International Standard on Auditing 315 (Redrafted) (2006), 'Identifying and assessing the risks of material misstatement through understanding the entity and its environment' in *ISAs 240, 300, 315 and 330 (Redrafted),* New York, NY, International Auditing and Assurance Standards Board; also available online at http://www.ifac.org/Members/DownLoads/IAASB-RD-ISAS-RedraftedISAs.pdf (accessed 1 November 2010).

International Standard on Auditing (UK and Ireland) (ISA (UK and Ireland)) 610, 'Using the work of internal auditors', available from http://www.frc.org.uk/images/uploaded/documents/ISA%20(UK%20and%20Ireland)%20610%20(final)%20.pdf (accessed 1 November 2010).

Jensen, M.C. and Meckling, W.H. (1976) 'Theory of the firm: managerial behavior, agency costs and ownership structure', *Journal of Financial Economics*, vol. 3, no. 4, pp. 305–60.

Law, J. and Owen, G. (eds) (1999) *A Dictionary of Accounting*, Oxford, Oxford University Press; available from Oxford Reference Online at http://www.oxfordreference.com/views/ENTRY.html?subview=Main&entry=t17.e3087 (accessed 7 October 2009).

Lord Burns (2008) Letter to Marks & Spencer shareholders, available from the B291 website.

Marks & Spencer (2009) *Code of Ethics*, London, Marks & Spencer, available from the B291 website.

Marks & Spencer (2007) 'Plan A' [online], http://plana.marksandspencer.com/about (accessed 14 October 2010).

Moore, M (2008) 'True and fair requirement revisited' [online], London, Financial Reporting Council, http://www.frc.org.uk/documents/pagemanager/frc/T&F%20Opinion%2021%20April%202008.pdf (accessed 14 October 2010).

OECD (2004) *OECD Principles of Corporate Governance*, Paris, OECD; also available online at http://www.oecd.org/dataoecd/32/18/31557724.pdf (accessed 31 August 2010).

Patsuris, P. (2002) 'The corporate scandal sheet' [online], *Forbes.com*, http://www.forbes.com/2002/07/25/accountingtracker_print.html (accessed 2 September 2010).

Siemens (2009) 'Corporate Governance report' [online], http://www.siemens.com/annual/09/pool/en/downloads/siemens_ar09_corpgov.pdf (accessed 14 October 2010).

Singer, P. (1985) 'Ethics' in *Encyclopaedia Britannica*, Chicago, pp. 627–48; available online at http://www.utilitarian.net/singer/by/1985.htm (accessed 12 May 2009).

Singer, P. (1997) *Practical Ethics* (2nd edn), Cambridge, Cambridge University Press, p. 317.

Skapinker, M. (2009) 'Why corporate responsibility is a survivor', *Financial Times*, 20 April.

Smith, A. (1776) *An Inquiry into the Nature and Causes of the Wealth of Nations* (often referred to by the short title *The Wealth of Nations*), Electric Book Company.

Smith, R. (2003) *Audit Committees: Combined Code Guidance*, London, Financial Reporting Council.

The Financial Express (2009) 'Satyam fraud: full text of Raju's letter to board', posted online 7 January, http://www.financialexpress.com/printer/news/407799/ (accessed 2 September 2010).

The UK Corporate Governance Code (2010), London, Financial Reporting Council; also available online at www.frc.org.uk.

Tran, M. (2002) 'WorldCom accounting scandal', *The Guardian*, 9 August, http://www.guardian.co.uk/business/2002/aug/09/corporatefraud.worldcom2 (accessed 2 September 2010).

Turnbull Review Group (2005) 'Turnbull Report' (full title: *Internal Control Revised Guidance for Directors on the Combined Code*), Financial Reporting Council, London, UK.

Walker, D. (2009) *A Review of Corporate Governance in UK Banks and Other Financial Industry Entities: Final Recommendations*, London, HM Treasury; also available online at http://www.hm-treasury.gov.uk/d/walker_review_261109.pdf (accessed 31 August 2010).

Verma, R. and Nuthall, K. (2009) 'Satyam fraud methodology revealed' [online], *Accountancy Age*, 29 April, http://www.accountancyage.com/articles/print/2241336 (accessed 2 September 2010).

Acknowledgements

Grateful acknowledgement is made to the following sources:

Cover image: © Pgiam/iStockphoto.com

Text

Page 45: Skapinker, M. (2009) 'Why corporate responsibility is a survivor', Financial Times, April 20 2010, Financial Times Syndication

Page 76: Raju, B.R. (2009) 'Satyam fraud: Full text of Raju's letter to the board'. The Indian Express Limited

Page 78: Verma, R. and Nuthall, K. 'Satyam fraud methodology revealed', Accountancy Age, 29 April 2009, www.accountancyage.com

Page 81: Tran, M. (2002) 'WorldCom accounting scandal', www.guardian.co.uk, 9 August 2002. Copyright Guardian News & Media Ltd 2002

Tables

Table 1: Carroll, A.B. (1991) 'The Pyramid of Corporate Social Responsibility: Toward the Moral Management of Organizational Stakeholders', in 'Business Horizons' Vol 34, Issue 4, July/August 1991. © 1991 Elsevier

Page 68: Patsuris, P. (2002) 'The corporate scandal sheet', www.forbes.com, 26 August 2002. Reprinted by Permission of Forbes Media LLC © 2010

Illustrations

Page 13: © Jim Sizemore, www.CartoonStock.com

Page 17: © iStockphoto.com/JOE CICAK

Page 64: With kind permission from Philip Talbot

Page 72: 'Frankly, Mr Clause, we don't understand...' © Noel Ford, www.CartoonStock.com

Page 79: © Tribune Media Services, Inc. All Rights Reserved. Reprinted with permission

Every effort has been made to contact copyright holders. If any have been inadvertently overlooked the publishers will be pleased to make the necessary arrangements at the first opportunity.